It's A Matter Of Faith And Life
Volume 1

A Catechism Companion

Baptism,
Confession, Absolution,
The Office Of The Keys,
And Holy Communion

David M. Albertin

CSS Publishing Company, Inc., Lima, Ohio

IT'S A MATTER OF FAITH AND LIFE — VOLUME 1

Copyright © 1997 by
CSS Publishing Company, Inc.
Lima, Ohio

All rights reserved. No part of this publication may be reproduced in any manner whatsoever without the prior permission of the publisher, except in the case of brief quotations embodied in critical articles and reviews. Inquiries should be addressed to: Permissions, CSS Publishing Company, Inc., P.O. Box 4503, Lima, Ohio 45802-4503.

Scripture quotations are from the *Revised Standard Version of the Bible*, copyrighted 1946, 1952 ©, 1971, 1973, by the Division of Christian Education of the National Council of the Churches of Christ in the USA. Used by permission.

Some scripture quotations are from the *Holy Bible, New International Version*. Copyright © 1973, 1978, 1984 International Bible Society. Used by permission of Zondervan Bible Publishers. All rights reserved.

From Luther's *Small Catechism*, 1986, Copyright 1986 Concordia Publishing House. Used with permission.

Library of Congress Cataloging-in-Publication Data

Albertin, David M., 1939-
   It's a matter of faith and life / David M. Albertin.
     p.   cm.
   Contents: v. 1. Baptism, confession, absolution, the office of the keys, and holy communion — v. 2. The Apostles' creed and the Lord's prayer — v. 3. The Ten commandments.
     ISBN 0-7880-0356-9 (pbk. : v. 1). — ISBN 0-7880-0357-7 (pbk. : v. 2). — ISBN 0-7880-0358-5 (pbk. : v. 3)
   1. Luther, Martin, 1483-1546. Kleine Katechismus. 2. Lutheran Church—Catechisms—English. I. Title.
BX8070.L8A7   1997
238'.41—DC21
                                          96-47408
                                                CIP

ISBN 0-7880-0356-9   Book, Vol. 1.   PRINTED IN U.S.A.

To my three children
Timothy
Jonathan
Kristen
and their children

Table Of Contents

Preface — 7

Baptism: Part One — 11

Baptism: Part Two — 17
   Why Do We Baptize?

Baptism: Part Three — 23
   The Blessings And Power Of Baptism

Baptism: Part Four — 29
   What Does Baptism Signify?

Confession — 37

Absolution — 45

The Office Of The Keys — 53

Holy Communion: Part One — 63

Holy Communion: Part Two — 71

Holy Communion: Part Three — 77

Holy Communion: Part Four — 83

Preface

It's A Matter Of Faith And Life originally appeared in the form of a script for a television program *(The Lutheran Lexicon)* which appeared on the Michigan City, Indiana, ecumenical community access cable channel. It also has been employed in the catechetical instruction of junior high youth at Immanuel Lutheran Church of Michigan City.

In its present form *It's A Matter Of Faith And Life* appears as a narrative companion to Dr. Martin Luther's *Small Catechism*. It is written in a style that should be attractive to readers of all ages.

Each chapter of *It's A Matter Of Faith And Life* focuses on a part of the *Small Catechism*. For example, there is a chapter on Baptism Part One, the Second Article of the Apostles' Creed, the Third Commandment, the Fourth Petition of the Lord's Prayer, and so forth. Each of these chapters does not exhaust the content of what the Catechism has to say. Rather the chapters focus on a key and significant issue that underlies the particular part being discussed.

It's A Matter Of Faith And Life, this book of words about words which ultimately focuses on the Word, can be employed as a devotional reader or as a supplement to the Catechism in catechetical instruction. The biblical quotes have been taken from the Revised Standard Version of the Bible. Some of them, however, are my own liberal translations and summaries. The references to the *Small Catechism* have been taken from the 1986 edition of *Luther's Small Catechism With Explanation,* Concordia Publishing House, St. Louis, Missouri.

The material in *It's A Matter Of Faith And Life* reflects my five decades of being a Christian. These pages began to be formed by the influence of my parents and the church which I attended as a child. The many references and examples cited have been gleaned from my childhood experiences, the Christian instructors at whose feet I have sat, my own reading and studying, and from what I have encountered as an adult and a pastor. Therefore, precise documentation and citing of sources is frequently absent. Instead, I would like to thank all of those who have had an effect on my Christian formation: my parents, my Sunday School teachers, my various instructors at the three Concordias I attended, and my friends both on the "street" and of the academic.

In other words, this is a book about life, the life of a Christian, and how the six chief parts of the Christian faith as presented in the *Small Catechism* of Dr. Martin Luther interacted with his life and gave shape and direction to it.

God be thanked for the numerous and wonderful ways He has provided for my Christian pilgrimage and growing in the faith. These pages have been written to share with you some of that which has been shared with me.

Soli Deo Gloria

David Albertin
Michigan City, Indiana
Winter 1996

Baptism

Baptism: Part One

This book in three parts, *It's A Matter Of Faith And Life: A Catechism Companion*, speaks about the Christian faith as Lutherans confess it.

There are all sorts of "faith and life" and "life and death" issues in life. Many of them are dependent upon choices that we make ranging all the way from the use of drugs and alcohol, to what to do about a pregnancy, to what to do about an elderly person who is seriously ill, to educational and vocational goals, to attending or not attending church, to being honest at school and at home. Before you go on with the rest of this chapter, identify some "faith and life" and some "life and death" issues that you have faced or are facing.

Lutherans have another book, this one written by Dr. Martin Luther, the sixteenth century reformer, which also speaks about the Christian faith as many of us confess it. It is a book which presents the chief doctrines, the chief messages, of the Book of Books, the Bible. Dr. Luther called his book the *Small Catechism.* It is called "Small" because it is not very big. It is called a "Catechism" because....

A Catechism is a book which is presented in a Question and Answer form. First, a question is asked, and then an answer is given. For example, first the question:

What is Baptism?

Then the answer:

*Baptism is not water only,
but it is water used together with God's Word and by His command.*

❖ ❖ ❖ ❖ ❖

The "Socratic method" (named after the ancient Greek philosopher Socrates) aims at getting at truth by repeatedly asking questions. For example, a question is asked. An answer is given. Another question is asked, usually related in some way to the previous answer. An answer is given, and so the process continues. A catechism, like Martin Luther's *Small Catechism,* is arranged somewhat that way. Try the Socratic method. With someone else pursue a "faith and life" or "life and death" question and answer exercise where each question is linked with the preceding answer. Make sure that the questions probe and clarify previous answers. Some possible topics are: the present state of morality in the U.S., the quality of education in our schools, or what is justice. For example: Q. What is life? A. Life is more than breathing. Q. In what way is life more than breathing? A. Really living is having purpose in life. Q. What is meant by purpose?

❖ ❖ ❖ ❖ ❖

I begin this book with a discussion of Baptism, because that is usually where the Christian faith begins for a lot of people.

❖ ❖ ❖ ❖ ❖

What are some of the different churches that you have visited or attended? What were some of the distinctive differences between them? In the following paragraphs you are going to be taken to three different churches. As you read these words, visualize each of them. Try also to identify the three different denominations that each represents. In your mind, add some music. Hum it while reading.

❖ ❖ ❖ ❖ ❖

Imagine, if you will, this scene: On a hot midsummer's Sunday afternoon, two cars pull up in front of an awe-inspiring grey stone building in a large eastern city. As the people step from their automobiles, they smooth their clothing and then begin to climb the steps that lead to the main entrance of this building, which, by the way, has a high steeple towering over it. The steeple has a cross on top of it. They are met at the door by a priest dressed in a colorful robe. He leads them into the cool, vaulted nave of the church. Once they are there, the people present are arranged so that they stand before a beautifully carved stone basin which has water in it. The priest says some prayers in a language which the people do not understand, and then he sprinkles some of the water from the basin onto the head of an infant only a few days old, saying softly, "Ego baptizo te in nomine Patris, et Filii, et Spiritus Sancti." Soon the ceremony is over. There are the cordial handshakes with accompanying smiles. Then the neatly dressed folks with the little baby walk back out of the church, climb into their cars, and drive off again into the heat of the afternoon, thinking of the party at which they will soon refresh themselves.

Or, perhaps this is the scene: On a fresh spring evening, in a theater-like building in southern California, thousands of people have been assembled already for nearly an hour. They are singing, sometimes shouting, and listening to religious music which has a distinct rhythmic beat. Now it is time for the climactic event of the evening. Above a cleverly rigged hydraulic stage, a curtain is drawn back. There, at the very top of the building, bathed in green light, sparkles a glass-walled tank of water. The crowd begins to hum, "Just as I am without one plea," and so forth. Slowly, from either side of the pool, a minister and a woman, both in white robes, descend the stairs which lead into the water. "Do you believe in Jesus Christ as your personal Savior?" asks the minister. "Yes," gasps the woman. The minister then covers the woman's nose and mouth with his hand, places his arm behind her back, and lowers her into the green-lit water three times. He is careful to immerse her completely each time. "I baptize you in the name of the Father, and of the Son, and of the Holy Ghost," he says. Both of them then leave the tank, and the service continues with a renewed source of energy.

Or, maybe this is the scene: Anywhere in the country on any Sunday, the congregation, dressed in its Sunday best, has assembled for morning worship. But on this Sunday everybody present senses something a bit special. A proud young couple, their first baby, and two close Christian friends are seated in the front row waiting for the service to begin. Very soon, at a special place in the worship service, an usher comes forward, and the pastor steps to the baptismal font, a stand with a basin of water in it. The baby's parents and their two close friends, sponsors, then step forward with the youngster in the arms of one of the friends; she is a lady and is called the godmother. If you watch carefully and listen closely to what is happening and being said, you'll notice something odd: the pastor is addressing questions to the tiny infant who is only a few days old. But, since the infant cannot answer for itself, the questions are being answered by the godparents just as if the baby itself were speaking.

"Do you desire to be baptized?"

"I do," the godparents respond.

"Do you renounce all the forces of evil, the devil, and all his empty promises?"

Again, the child's sponsors (the godparents) respond, "I do!"

The questions continue. The tiny one, hardly able to distinguish even its mother by sight or sound, is asked in all seriousness, "Do you believe in God the Father ... and the Son ... and the Holy Ghost?"

And as always, again the sponsors answer that as the Apostles' Creed confesses so the baby does believe.

Finally, the pastor motions for the godmother to hold the baby in such a way that its head is right over the basin of water. Then, he scoops the water from the basin with his hand and runs it over the head of the small child three times saying, "I baptize you in the name of the Father, and of the Son, and of the Holy Ghost. Amen."

What do you think might be some interesting additions to a baptismal ceremony that might lend it some special meaning? (For example, the hitting of nails into a piece of wood to remind us that we are baptized into Jesus' death.)

If you were to construct a baptismal ceremony, what would be among the ingredients? In fact, try your hand at putting together a baptismal ceremony. Give a reason for each of the separate parts. Think of making them memorable. What scripture references and passages would you include? But your ceremony should include more than words. For example, where (in a church or perhaps outside of a church) would you conduct the ceremony? How about the water? How much would you use? How would you apply it? Consider adding blooms or something similar to the ceremony. How would a baptism ceremony for an adult be different from a baptism ceremony for an infant? What would you have the congregation, those in attendance, do?

In all probability many of you have been baptized in one or the other of these three ways. Perhaps you were carried as an infant screaming and kicking to the front of the church to be baptized. Or maybe you were a teenager when you come to know Christ as your Savior and then were baptized in the name of the Triune God. Some people are already adults when this all happens. Chances are you have also seen someone baptized in at least one of these three ways. The point is, however it happens, regardless of the ceremony that accompanies it, baptism, the taking of water and accompanying it with the word of God in the name of the Triune God, Father, the Son, and the Holy Ghost, is for the forgiveness of sins. And so in all three scenes which I asked you to visualize, Christians, in response to their Lord's command, were taking water in His name and applying it to persons as a sign and seal of their now being the forgiven sons and daughters of the Kingdom of God.

When was the most recent Baptism that you can remember? What do you remember most about it?

Remembering gives life meaning. What are some of the most memorable events from your life? Do you remember your baptism? When were you baptized: as an infant, as a teenager, or as an adult? If you can remember the event, what was it like? What do you remember most about it?

It all began some 2,000 years ago when a rather unusual event took place in Jerusalem of Judea in the year 33 A.D. That had in many respects been a rather unusual year. Most noteworthy was that a man claiming to be God had been crucified. That's not unusual in itself. History records the stories of many men who were executed for similar reasons. But this man, it was also reported by those who saw him, actually came back to life. And then, if that were not enough, He, a few weeks after His resurrection, actually ascended up into the sky. He literally and visually left this earth in the presence of a whole host of eyewitnesses who said that He had returned to heaven from

❖ ❖ ❖ ❖❖

Imagine being in Jerusalem 2,000 years ago at the time of Pentecost. What do you suppose would have been your reaction to the sights and sounds of that day? (Compare yourself to the reaction of the people who were there: Acts 2.) Do you think that you would have been among the scoffers or among the 3,000 baptized? Why? Why not?

❖ ❖ ❖ ❖ ❖

which He had come. Ten days later, the followers of this man, called His "disciples," were huddled together in a room in Jerusalem, afraid that they might be the next to be arrested and also hung up on a cross and executed. (All of that is recorded in the second chapter of "The Acts of the Apostles," the fifth book of the New Testament.) On this tenth day another unusual event took place. First, there was the sound of a mighty rushing wind. But the trees did not move. Then, the men called "disciples" seemed to glow, just as if they were on fire. But, of course, they weren't. And then they all began to talk, to preach, in all sorts of different languages. These were languages that they had never spoken before. Finally, one of them, Peter by name, commanded the attention of all those who could hear him. He preached a marvelous sermon about the life, death, and resurrection of Jesus the Christ. And, by the power of that Holy Spirit who was directing the events of that day, thousands who heard him were deeply moved. They asked Peter what they should. Peter answered, "Repent (get a change of heart) and be baptized, every one of you, in the name of Jesus Christ for the forgiveness of your sins; and you too shall receive the gift of the Holy Spirit." Three thousand responded that day by being baptized. And people have been baptized ever since: millions and billions of them.

All of this is also in response to what the church calls "The Great Commission." For that we now turn to the concluding verses of Matthew 28. Jesus, immediately before He ascended into heaven, said to His assembled disciples, "Therefore go and make disciples of all nations, baptizing them in the name of the Father and of the Son and of the Holy Spirit."

That is a commission! Those are words of instruction!

There are a lot of "commissions" in life: things that we are told to do. What are some of your "commissions"? For example, what are some of the things that are expected of you at home, at school, at work, in your community, and at church (such as feeding the cat — home; doing your homework — school; being on time — work; paying taxes — community; being friendly — church)? Which of them seem important? Which of them do not seem to be very important?

Detail a plan which you think would be good for "making disciples of all nations." How do you think the job should be done? What are some of the things that you could do in this respect?

❖ ❖ ❖ ❖ ❖

As we saw earlier, Martin Luther begins his discussion of Baptism in the *Small Catechism* by asking the simple question, "What is Baptism?" Then he answers the question. Then another question is asked: "Which is that word of God?" And it too is followed by an answer. Remember? A Catechism is a book, a teaching book, of questions and answers.

Finally, I personally am thankful that I had parents who stood in the long tradition of the apostles and saw to it that in response to Christ's commission to them I was baptized. Now **I am baptized**, and from the very early moments of my life I have been a receiver of God's grace and mercy.

I would like to talk more about that with you in the next chapter.

There is a subtle but important distinction between "having BEEN baptized" and "BEING baptized." Identify the distinction. In this respect, set your mind to do something before the day is over which reflects your "being baptized."

❖ ❖ ❖ ❖ ❖

Questions

1. What is the nature of a Catechism?

2. What happened on Pentecost?

3. What is the "Great Commission"?

4. When were you baptized? Where were you baptized? How were you baptized?

Discussion

1. Compare the three ways of baptizing which were referred to in this chapter.

2. Discuss the nature of the Great Commission and what influence it has on your life.

Baptism: Part Two

Why Do We Baptize?

Family get-togethers, reunions, and celebrations are important for family life. Make a quick list of all these sorts of family gatherings your family has had in the last twelve months. (Include weddings, birthdays, funerals, holidays and so forth.) On a scale of 1 to 10, rate the importance of each of these gatherings. Then total the rating numbers and divide by the number of events for the average score.

Also make a list of special events celebrated by your church within the past twelve months. As you did above, rate each event and then find the average score. (Include special anniversaries, holiday worship services, groundbreaking, and so forth.)

When a child is baptized, it is customary for the whole family to get together — grandpas and grandmas, uncles and aunts, brothers, sisters and cousins. It is time for a celebration, and the center of attention is the little infant attired in a white dress or suit. The baptism itself takes perhaps only a few minutes, but the celebration most likely will go on for hours. I suppose that is okay, because baptism happens only once in a person's life, and like being born it means living, living a new life. It is the creation of new life.

But baptism also means death and dying. A baptism is something like a funeral, a time when the whole family gets together again. We say that baptism is something like a funeral, because for Christians baptism in many ways is the visible and public break with the world, with the old way of living. Yes, it is like dying to the world and being born again into the Kingdom of God.

Therefore, baptism since the days of the apostles has been one of the hallmarks of the Christian church. One can hardly think of the church without also thinking of baptism. One can hardly think of the Christian faith without thinking of baptism. It is such an essential part of the Christian's and the church's life.

On a scale of 1 to 10, rate how important baptisms seem to be at your church.

Why is this so? Why is baptism such an important part of the Christian way of life? Why do Christians place such an importance on baptism? The answer to these questions is really quite simple: We baptize because our Lord, Jesus the Christ, told us to do so.

Is it not true that a person's last words (his or her last will and testament of sorts) are generally considered to be among the most important? Many times we ask, or at least are curious about, what was the last thing a person said, either (sadly) before he died, or perhaps before she left on a long trip. We hang on to those words. We attach significance to them. And so also with the last will and testament, the last words, of Jesus.

Famous last words: jot some down, even if they are not so famous and even if the person who said them is not so famous and even if the words were not the absolutely last words spoken by that person. But make sure that they are words by which the person who spoke them is remembered. The Bible also has numerous "last words" spoken by God's leaders. Check who said what: Genesis 49; the entire book of Deuteronomy; 1 Kings 2:1-4; Revelation 22:18-21. In each case focus on how important the words were.

After His resurrection and before His ascension, Jesus spent forty days with His disciples. At the end of those days He gathered them around Himself, and immediately before He ascended to heaven He gave them a command (some instructions) which we call "The Great Commission."

Certainly we must confess that everything that Jesus said and which is recorded by the Evangelists is important. We more or less hang on to every word. How can we then say that some of the words are more important than others? I suppose that it all depends upon the purpose for which the words were spoken. These last words of Jesus were spoken in order to give direction to the ministry of the apostles. These words have a lot to say about that. They surely do have a ring of importance to them.

We baptize because Jesus told us to, and that baptizing has always been, then, an important part of the church's ministry. So let's look carefully once more at the words of "The Great Commission." Christ, our Lord, says in the last chapter of Matthew that we are to go and make disciples of all nations, baptizing them in the name of the Father and of the Son and of the Holy Ghost (Spirit).

In the Lutheran Church, as well as in those churches which have through the ages stood in the mainstream of Christian history, the words "all nations" are interpreted to mean and include males, females, big people, little people, white and black and brown and yellow and red people, people with blue eyes and those with brown eyes, older folks and younger folks, adults, children, and even infants. Now I would like to tell you why it has meant that.

It appears that the first Christians to be baptized were all adults, and all male adults at that. They were baptized on the day called Pentecost; it was on that day that the Holy Spirit was "poured out" upon the teaching and preaching of the disciples. It took place ten days after the Ascension of Jesus. Thousands had gathered in Jerusalem in order to celebrate Pentecost, a Jewish Spring Harvest festival. Many of them heard the disciples preach and teach on that day in all sorts of languages — all the languages that these men spoke in their homelands.

It appears that at the time of Pentecost (Acts 2) most of the "pilgrims" in Jerusalem were men. It also appears from much of the church's early history that men (fathers) were responsible for the spiritual life of their families. Is it the same today? What about families where there is no father to take a lead? What about the example of Lydia (Acts 16:11-15)? What about 1 Peter 3:1-2?

You might wonder, "But where were the women and the children? Why weren't they there? Today they come to church and hear preaching and teaching just as do the men." Well, you see, in those days (in Bible times) usually only men gathered for worship. Most of the women and children stayed home. It was the duty of the men to be teachers of religion to their families. Therefore, as you might imagine, those men who on Pentecost believed and were baptized now went home and saw to it that the rest of the members of their families also came to know Jesus and were baptized. The Book of the Acts of the Apostles has a number of such cases. For example, in Acts 16 we read the story of Cornelius. This is exactly what happened in his family, and history tells us over and over again that in the days of the early church when an adult man sought the Christian faith, he usually was first instructed, then baptized, and then his entire family would follow the lead of the man of the house. If he was of "the Family of Faith" the members of his family also became members of "the Family of Faith" — by baptism.

But you might still wonder, "But why baptize little children when they cannot even understand what is happening to them?"

I would like to share with you an analogy, a comparison: when a person immigrates to this country, let's say from Germany or Brazil or Korea, that person, before he or she can become a citizen of this country, must take instruction in what citizenship is all about. The idea is that he or she should learn about the rights, responsibilities, and privileges of citizenship before it is granted. However, to a person who is born in this country of parents who already are citizens, the gift of citizenship is automatically given. I, for example, became an American citizen on August 27, 1939. And there were no questions asked. However, at the time I became a citizen of this country all the rights and privileges of citizenship were not yet mine. Instead, it was decided for me that I go to school and that there I should learn how to read and write so that I might eventually become a mature person, a law-abiding citizen, and a person who could make a contribution to the commonwealth — my community. And it was only after I had attained a certain level of maturity and a certain age that I was granted the right to drive an automobile and vote. However, if I violate what my country expects of me, then I stand to lose some of the privileges that have been given to me. Yes, if I break certain laws, I might even find myself behind locked bars. No longer at liberty to come and go as I please, and, of course, I would lose my right to vote.

Citizenship carries with it both privileges and responsibilities. Make two lists: one of citizenship's privileges and one of citizenship's responsibilities. If that is true of national citizenship, is it also true of spiritual citizenship? If you think that it is, again make two lists, only this time identify the privileges and the responsibilities of citizenship in the Kingdom of God.

Similarly, little children who are baptized in the faith do not understand the faith. However, those little children are not baptized into a vacuum. They are baptized into a family, a family of faith, the members of which are responsible for raising these children in the faith and for educating them in the faith, so that when they are more mature they can understand what it is like to live as Christians.

In order for children to grow up responsibly, they are required to go to school. What are some of the things that you think a good education should provide? What are some of the things that you think a good religious education should provide? Also propose how this "good education" (public and church) could be accomplished.

Now, that does not mean that a person being a Christian is dependent only upon his or her understanding of what a Christian is. For many years I didn't even know what it was to be an

American. At first I hardly understood what it meant to be a part of my family. But I was just as much a part of it then as I am now! Likewise, I was a Christian from the moment of my youthful baptism on, even though at that time I did not understand what it was all about.

There is another reason why we believe so firmly in the baptizing of all nations, of all people. We believe, teach, and confess that all people are born sinners. All of us since Adam and Eve have inherited this terminal disease, this fatal illness. It is called "original sin." King David in Psalm 51 confessed, "Behold, I was brought forth in iniquity, and in sin did my mother conceive me."

Water has numerous purposes. Identify as many of them as you can. Did you list any purposes which are purely negative? Water can be both a blessing and a curse. It can be both an agent for life and an agent for death.

Psalm 51 is considered to be a Penitential Psalm. Refer to 2 Samuel 11 and 12 for the historical background to this Psalm. Have you ever felt like King David? Look carefully at Psalm 51. How closely do you identify with it? Or do you think that people by nature are good or at least neutral and that evil is something acquired and learned? Refer also to Romans 7:15-20. Do you ever feel like Paul?

Even if we did not have the Scriptures to tell us so, we would be able to observe that sin is not something we only can learn. It just seems to be there right from the beginning, right from the start. Yes, we might learn more sophisticated ways of sinning as we grow older, but we don't need much encouragement in beginning to do it.

A famous psychiatrist, Karl Menninger, once observed:

> *Children between the ages of one and two when put together in a playpen, will bite each other, pull each other's hair, and rob each other's toys, without regard for the other child's happiness ... If we observe young children at play, we notice they will destroy their toys, pull off the arms and legs of their dolls ... smash whatever is breakable ... The more their independence and strength are growing, the more they have to be watched so as not to create too much damage.*

The point is, we all need a Savior, someone to deliver us from all this violence and hurt. As Saint Paul wrote, "All have sinned and have fallen short of the law, of what God expects." And that includes young and old alike, blonds and brunettes, grandmas and grandpas, moms, dads, brothers, sisters, cousins, and little babies too.

However, baptism is not given to us in order to remind us how bad we are. Baptism is a gift given to us to remind us of how good God is! Thus, in this wonderful sacrament, God has provided a way in which we all can be loved by His grace — little ones among us and big ones, too.

In summary then, the Christian church baptizes because Jesus has told us to do so. That is what is called "The Great Commission." We also baptize because down through the years the church always has, and we stand in its long line of tradition. Finally, we baptize because we are all in need of what it has to offer — the washing away of our sins. It gives us forgiveness.

Questions

1. When was your funeral?

2. How is Baptism like birth and death all wrapped into one?

3. When did you become a citizen of the USA?

4. What do we call the sins with which we are born?

5. What are the three reasons for baptizing?

6. What does it mean that "all nations" are to be baptized?

Discussion

1. Discuss the parallels between being baptized and having citizenship in a country.

2. How does your church go about helping young people understand what being baptized means for living?

3. Dr. Karl Menninger speaks about how "rough" infants can be. Discuss the kind of behavior he describes with what you have witnessed.

4. Do you remember the "last words" of someone? What were they? How important were they?

Baptism: Part Three

The Blessings And Power Of Baptism

❖ ❖ ❖ ❖ ❖

There are many versions of the "rat race." The rat race is often identified as life that is very, very busy but which does not seem to have any purpose to it. Identify some of the busyness in your life that you are experiencing at the present. Some can be very important. Some can be very meaningless. Decide which busyness should receive more of your attention and which busyness should be reduced.

Can you think of anyone else whose life is very, very busy? Do you see that busyness as having a purpose, or is it simply eating up (consuming) that person?

❖ ❖ ❖ ❖ ❖

"Alas," said the mouse, "the world is growing smaller every day. At the beginning it was so big that I was afraid; I kept running and running, and I was glad when at last I saw walls far away to the right and to the left, but those walls have narrowed so quickly that I am in the last chamber already, and there in the corner stands the trap into which I must run."

"You only need to change your direction," said the cat, who then pounced on and ate the mouse.

With that little story we continue our discussion of the Sacrament of Holy Baptism. However, you might be thinking to yourself, "Cute little story about the cat and the mouse, but what in the world does it have to do with Baptism?"

This: the poor mouse ran into a dead end. His version of the "rat race" ended when he became food for the cat, never more again to be heard from, and never more again to be seen.

People like you and me sometimes feel that way. Would that there would be something to save us from such a meaningless fate.

There is! For Christians believe, teach, and confess that they are indeed called to a much more significant destiny by the washing of the water with the Word in Holy Baptism.

> **What are some of your "Christian" activities? Are they important, or do they seem to be meaningless? For example, some of these activities might include going to church, reading the Bible, being a part of a group at church, serving on a committee, and so forth. Ask yourself, "Why am I doing these things?" Ask yourself, "What should I be doing?"**

In the last chapter we looked at Martin Luther's answer to the question, "What is Baptism?" Now we will look at another question and its answer. The question is, "What benefits does Baptism give?" Again from Luther's *Small Catechism* comes the answer:

> *It works forgiveness of sins, rescues from death and the devil, and gives eternal salvation to all who believe this, as the words and promises of God declare.*
>
> *Which are these words and promises of God?*
>
> *Christ our Lord says in the last chapter of Mark: "Whoever believes and is baptized will be saved, but whoever does not believe will be condemned."*

> **Today we consider it very important that there be a reason for doing things. What are some of the things in life which you do which seem to be important? What are some of the things which you do which seem to be rather unimportant?**

The question is frequently asked, "Why baptize? What good is it?" Well, as you can now see, the answer to those questions is given to us in this portion of Martin Luther's *Small Catechism*. We baptize so that we might have the forgiveness of sins. That also means that when we have this forgiveness we are set free from the fate that the devil has waiting for us: death. Instead we now are the receivers of that life and salvation which God has waiting for us.

❖ ❖ ❖ ❖ ❖
Why do people die? (See Genesis 3 and Romans 6:23.) If sin is taken away what will then be the result? According to "the last chapter of Mark" how do we get hold of "everlasting life"?
❖ ❖ ❖ ❖ ❖

The people of the Old Testament times liked to compare being saved, "salvation," with being "set out into a large open space." Psalm 18:19 speaks of it this way. "He (the Lord) brought me forth into a broad place." The Psalmist, you see, is thanking God that he has been delivered from the hands of his enemies, that by God's protection he has escaped ambush. He has been set out into a large open place where he can protect himself against sneak attack, where he can see the enemy coming.

This reminds me of the cowboy and Indian movies I saw as a child. There always seemed to be Indians hiding behind rocks in those canyons through which every wagon train or calvary column had to pass. You knew that they, the Indians, were there. So you just waited until the ambush began, or you breathed a sigh of relief when and if the cowboys or soldiers made it safely through.

❖ ❖ ❖ ❖ ❖
There are many ways in which "being saved" (salvation) can be expressed. With the help of others, draw up a list of such expressions.
❖ ❖ ❖ ❖ ❖

This brings us back to the poor mouse with whose story we began this chapter. He got boxed in. He got trapped. And with no place to go, the cat simply ate him up.

Is it not so that often we too feel trapped in and by life? We find ourselves fenced in. We end up in dead ends. Would that we could be delivered.

We are! Our sins which have sealed our tombs are removed, and now the entrances to our graves can fly open. That's what Baptism does for us.

Do you not know that all of us who have been baptized into Christ Jesus were baptized into his death? We were buried therefore with him by baptism into death, so that as Christ was raised from the dead by the glory of the Father, we too might walk in the newness of life. — Romans 6:3-4

❖ ❖ ❖ ❖ ❖
Everyone wishes that some thing(s) would be different in his or her life. What are some of the things which you wish would be different in your life? How can you "start all over again" so that some of these changes might take place?
❖ ❖ ❖ ❖ ❖

Saint Paul in those words from Romans is actually telling us that if we have been baptized our funerals are already behind us. We need not worry about getting trapped by death or eaten up by the grave.

That's also what Jesus meant when He said to Nicodemus, one of the leaders of the Jewish community of his day:

> *"Truly, truly, I say to you, unless one is born anew, he cannot see the kingdom of God." Nicodemus said to him, "How can a man be born when he is old?" ... Jesus answered, "Truly, truly, I say to you, unless one is born of the water and the Spirit, he cannot enter the kingdom of God."* — John 3:3-5

Yes, Baptism is a water, a water of life. Without water life does not last long. Water is the universal agent of life. It is as important to life as is the air we breathe. And with it, empowered by the Word of God, we are reborn; we are brought forth into new life.

How much of the earth's surface is covered by water? How much (what percentage) of our bodies is water? In the semiarid regions of the Near East, blue and green are the most important of colors. Why do you suppose that is so? Why is it important to conserve water if there is so much of it? Why is it important to be concerned about the pollution of water if there is so much of it? What possible connection do these last two questions have with Baptism?

Another significant property of water is its ability to cleanse. And this is true also of the water of Baptism. When the disciples in the early days of the church preached those mighty moving sermons, many who heard them were so impressed that they asked, "What should we do?" Over and over again the Apostles responded by saying, "Arise and be baptized and wash away your sins." They remembered the prophet Isaiah saying, "Though your sins are like scarlet, they shall be as white as snow; though they are red like crimson, they shall become like wool" (Isaiah 1:18).

That is exactly what Martin Luther meant when in his *Catechism* he said that Baptism gives to us "the forgiveness of sins, rescues from death and the devil, and gives eternal salvation...." That is quite an offer.

Christians also have dreams and wishes about some things in their lives which they wish would be different. Many times these things are "behaviors." What are some of your behaviors which you wish would be different, changed, new?

Which brings us to the next question about Baptism in the *Catechism*. Again Luther asks, this time saying, "How can water do such great things?" It certainly must be awfully powerful water! Where can one find such water?

Actually, the power for Baptism is not in the water. Rather, it is in the Word. That is what Dr. Luther said in the *Catechism* in answer to the question, "How can water do such great things?"

> *Certainly not just water, but the word of God in and with the water does these things, along with the faith which trusts this word of God in the water. For without God's word the water is plain water and no Baptism. But with the word of God it is a Baptism, that is, a life-giving water, rich in grace and a washing of the new birth in the Holy Spirit.*

The Bible has great respect for the power of the Word. Refer to Genesis 1 and how the world and everything in it was created. Refer to John 1 and the importance of the "Word becoming Incarnate." Refer to Romans 10:14-17 and the relationship between the Word and faith.

Think of the power of words in your life. They come in both positive and negative ways. What are some the powerful positive words you have heard today? What are some of the powerful negative words you have heard today? What is the best thing you have heard today? What is the most important thing you have heard today?

Recently I was reading a devotion which was written in the German language. I like to read devotions in German, because I do not know the German language as well as I know English. Therefore, I have to read much more slowly, so that I can figure out and absorb the meaning of what I am reading. There is a blessing in that. For the words have more time to sink in, and consequently they sometimes end up meaning more than if I had read them swiftly in English. Well, this devotion made reference to the fact that we often rather thoughtlessly make all sorts of promises which we cannot keep. For one reason or the other, we tell people that they can count on us. But often, either because we are not able to, or because we have changed our minds, or for some other reason, we just don't deliver. We don't follow through.

Some times we say that a person's word is his or her bond. What does that mean? Think of some of the promises you have made but which you also broke. Think of some of the promises others have made to you and have broken. Think also of some of the important promises you have made which you plan on keeping. And think of some of the promises others have made to you which they have kept.

But not so with God. What He promises, He delivers. And He promises, "He that believes and is baptized shall be saved." Saint Peter reiterates, "Baptism ... now saves us, not as removal of dirt from the body, but as an appeal to God for a clear conscience through the resurrection of Jesus Christ" (1 Peter 3:21). By saying this Peter is saying that our consciences are cleared, cleaned, when our sins are forgiven. That is a promise.

We can trust that Word, that Word of promise! It was that same Word, that mighty Word of God, which created the universe. It is that same Word which holds it all together. That Word is God's life-giving and life-sustaining Word.

❖ ❖ ❖ ❖ ❖

What are some of the promises which God made which He kept? What are some of the promises of God which He has made to you which He has kept? Do you have trouble believing God's words of promise? How can a person's faith in God's promises be strengthened?

❖ ❖ ❖ ❖ ❖

That is so basic to the Christian faith: believing and trusting that Word of God. We can even go so far as to say that without that Word there is no faith. But thanks be to God that His Word comes to us in baptism bearing faith and working in our hearts.

Questions

1. What did Jesus tell Nicodemus?

2. What does it mean to "be born again"?

3. What does God promise in Baptism?

4. From where does baptism get its power to do what it promises to do?

Discussion

1. Do you sometimes feel as if your life is meaningless? If so, how? Discuss that with someone.

2. Reflect on and discuss the idea of being "set out into a large open space" and what that feels like.

3. Paul talks about walking "in the newness of life." What does that mean for your living?

4. Discuss some promises that you have made but which you did not keep.

Baptism: Part Four

What Does Baptism Signify?

Life seems to teach us to be careful about whom we trust. Why is this so? How have you personally been hurt by someone whom you trusted? Are there some times when you can't even trust yourself? What are some of those times?

We are not born "Trusters." We are not born "natural Trusters." In fact, much of the time most of us don't trust anybody. After all, life teaches us very quickly that you better be careful whom you trust. Maybe, just maybe, you can't trust anybody, not even yourself. Yes, you, we, may in fact prove to be our own worst enemies. So … "Whom can you trust?"

Trust me! Trust that what I have to say to you is the truth. After all, why would I lie? How do you know that I won't lie? Many of you don't even know me. How can you be sure that my word is trustworthy? How do you know that I know what I am talking about? Just because I say that I do?

Words often are the instruments by which an invitation to trust is made. What are some of the invitations to trust that have been extended to you? What Words of invitation to trust have been extended to you by God? In what ways does God say, "Trust me"?

Even though we seem to have so much trouble with trusting others, and even ourselves, it is still something that we would all like to do, as difficult as that might be. How good it is whenever we find someone whom we can trust, whose word is trustworthy. Sometimes we translate the word "trust" as "faith." We say that those whom we can trust are those in whom we have faith.

Lutherans teach, believe, and confess that it is by Baptism that we are brought into a trusting, a faith, relationship with God. However, if the truth is really to be known, I think that we would have to also confess that all too often that trust, that faith, into which we as Christians are baptized is a bit on the weak side. Indeed, that baptismal relationship we have with God often is found to be a bit faded, bleached out, as far as our daily living is concerned. We just are not as strong in our faith and trust as we might be expected to be.

❖ ❖ ❖ ❖ ❖
The question is asked, "Why are we not as trusting of God as we ought to be?" Why aren't we? What are some of the things which get in the way of our trusting?
❖ ❖ ❖ ❖ ❖

Why is that so? Why are we not as trusting of God as we ought to be? Why does our faith so often seem to waver? Could it be that Baptism really is not all that important, all that meaningful, as we thought it was? Perhaps we have overemphasized Baptism.

I don't think that the problem is with the gift, with Baptism. The problem really is with us; it is with us who are the receivers of the gift. You see, our faith, trust, often is sort of a fickle thing. It works very well when everything is going well. But there are a lot of times when everything is not going so well. That reminds me of a time when the disciples got into a boat with Jesus. It was a calm, peaceful, Galilean evening. They had decided to go for a boat ride. How good it was to have Jesus with them. And so they sailed off into the sunset with not a worry or care in their heads or on their minds. They had a lot of fair weather faith.

Then a storm came up. Out of nowhere it seemed to come. It roared down upon them. It really surprised them. It caught them off guard. You ought to have seen how quickly the disciples started to shake in their sandals. Those bold fishermen suddenly found that whatever confidence they had was washed overboard. The faith and trust with which they had entered the boat soon disappeared. And in a moment of panic, terror-struck, they violently shook Jesus and cried into His ear that they were sure that they were going to sink.

"O, you men of little faith," Jesus said as He bid the waves to cease and the storm to pass.

❖ ❖ ❖ ❖ ❖
Remember some times when some of your friends were only "fair weather friends." Identify also some of the times when you were just a "fair weather friend." What causes fair weather friendliness to happen?

**(Refer to the disciples in the boat in the storm-tossed Sea of Galilee.)
Now list some of the storms in life that you have encountered. What
effect have they had on your relationship to God?**

❖ ❖ ❖ ❖ ❖

In life we too find that many storms interrupt what we had hoped would be a peaceful day. In life we too, just like the disciples, find it easy to be filled with all sorts of faith and confidence and trust when things are going well. But when the clouds assemble, like the disciples, we too panic. And that is precisely why I am glad that I am baptized. And that is what being baptized is all about; that is what it means for daily living. It is for the good times and for the storm-tossed times.

In the *Catechism* Martin Luther asks:

What does such baptizing with water indicate?

And he answers his own question:

It indicates that the Old Adam in us should by daily contrition and repentance be drowned and die with all sins and evil desires, and that a new man should daily emerge and arise to live before God in righteousness and purity forever.

And then he asks again:

Where is this written?

And he again answers his own question:

Saint Paul writes in Romans chapter six: "We were therefore buried with Him through baptism into death in order that, just as Christ was raised from the dead through the glory of the Father, we too may live a new life." — Romans 6:4

Those words are the fourth and last portion of Martin Luther's comments on the Sacrament of Holy Baptism. Those words speak to us of what Baptism means for our daily living — fair weather and foul weather living, for good days and especially for those days when the storms hit.

❖ ❖ ❖ ❖ ❖

**"Remembering" our baptisms can help us when we are threatened by
the storms of life. Making the sign of the cross might be one of the ways
to remember your baptism. What might be some appropriate times
and occasions for making the sign of the cross?**

❖ ❖ ❖ ❖ ❖

In Christ I have my life. In Him I have new life. And that means to me that even though my faith and trust in God may be weak at any particular moment, my God and Lord is always faithfully there, sustaining, caring for, counseling my soul. My faith may be weak, but His love is strong.

When I get up in the morning I have the habit of making the sign of the cross. I do so in order to remind myself that when I get up in the morning I am rising as a Christian, as a person who has been baptized into the life, death, and resurrection of Jesus Christ. And there is no finer symbol of that than the cross. Thus, I am reminded that all day long I can claim my baptismal faith and walk (live) like a redeemed, born-again son of God. That cross reminds me of from where has come my faith and in what I place it.

In the evening, when I lie down to sleep, I make the sign of the cross again. It says to me that as a baptized child of God, I am forgiven for all of my sins that willingly or unwillingly, knowingly or unknowingly, I have committed during the day. It reminds me that I am forgiven precisely because of Jesus, who died on a cross much like the one I just traced in the air over my heart. Yes, that cross reminds me that I can lie down in peace. Nothing need disturb my conscience as I place myself into the hands of the Almighty Father.

You see, what happened to me many, many years ago (before I even knew that it was happening) still has significance for me. Indeed, what happened then still has a great effect on what's happening now. I suppose that is why some have said, "Don't say 'I was baptized.' Say, 'I am baptized.' " You see, the effect of what happened once is still going on. It influences both my waking and my sleeping moments.

Being a member of a group, just like being a citizen of a nation, carries with it certain responsibilities. What are some of the responsibilities you carry as a member of your family, an athletic team, a club or organization, and so forth? (Identify those groups to which you belong and then list some of the responsibilities that are yours as a member.) Also, what are some of the responsibilities of citizenship that you have?

Yes, I must admit that those who say, "Just being baptized doesn't really mean anything," have a point. If a person lives as if his or her baptism doesn't really mean anything, then it really doesn't. It's much as if a citizen of the United States didn't really care about living like a citizen of the United States. In that case, his citizenship obviously would not mean very much. The test for the quality of meaning is in the living. That is why Saint Paul in the well-known sixth chapter of his letter to the Romans wrote, "How can we who died to sin still live in it? ... Therefore, you must consider yourself dead to sin and alive to God in Christ Jesus." Those are important words, because, you see, my faith and the exercise of it is often not as strong as I would like it to be. I have fears. I have mistrust. I sometimes even wonder if God really cares, if He is really looking out after me. And to make matters worse, I sometimes just go off in my own direction with little or no regard for how God would have me to live.

God has said, "Be dead to sin. Sin no more. Be not faithless."

Nevertheless, I find that very difficult. I find it very difficult to be as faithful as He would like me to be. The "newness of life" which Paul calls for seems to be a lot of "old" stuff. My new life is all too often very much like my old life. Baptism just doesn't seem to do that much for me. It does not seem to have much of an effect on the way I live. How can it save me from all of that, all of that "old" stuff?

Being a Christian carries with it certain responsibilities regarding behavior. Be precise, and identify at least ten behaviors which are fitting for Christians. In contrast, list ten behaviors which are not fitting for Christians. Make sure your lists include items from both your private and public life.

Listen: The good news is that those of us who are baptized are alive in God through Jesus Christ even though we sometimes feel half dead. The very sure word of promise is, "Do you not know that all of us who were baptized into Christ Jesus, were baptized into His death? ... So that as He was raised from the dead ... we too might walk in newness of life" (Romans 6:3-4). Those are words that we can trust.

Paul says in Romans 6:3-4 that we should "walk in newness of life." However, in Romans 7:15-25 he talks about how hard it is to do that. Look at these passages and reflect upon what they imply. They will give you some appreciation for the tough task it is to live like a Christian.

Christ was crucified to cover our sins and our faithlessness and to set us free from their terrible and eternal consequences. So by my baptism I have put on Christ like a new suit of clothing. It, He, covers me. And that covering includes all of my blemishes, my weaknesses, and my faithlessness.

I remember how it was as a child whenever I got a new pair of shoes. New shoes were rather difficult to come by then. And there were no such things as sneakers. A shiny new pair of shoes had to last a long time. And to make them last a long time my mother made me polish them regularly, at least every Saturday night. Well, I remember that whenever I got a new pair of shoes I was proud as a peacock to wear them. I was sure that everybody noticed: "He's got a new pair of shoes!" And, oh, a new suit of clothes: that made me feel as if the whole world was staring at me.

❖ ❖ ❖ ❖ ❖

"Clothes make the man," they say. How we dress often has a profound effect upon our behavior. Imagine yourself dressed in the following ways (consider how what you are wearing might affect your behavior): jeans and sneakers, swimsuit, formal clothing, church clothes, sweat suit.

Wearing Jesus like clothing has two effects: 1) it affects the way God the Father looks at us, and 2) it affects the way we act. How so? What does God the Father see when He sees us clothed with Christ by baptism? How does "wearing" Jesus affect our behavior?

❖ ❖ ❖ ❖ ❖

Those kinds of memories speak loudly to me when I think of Luther's fourth and final question and answer about Baptism: "What does such baptizing with water indicate?" ("What does Baptism mean for daily living?") It means that because of my Baptism I can wear Jesus like a new suit of clothes every day.

You'd be surprised what kind of confidence that gives me. That confidence can be translated as faith and trust in God.

Questions

1. The word "trust" is very similar to what other word?

2. When are we brought into a faith relationship with God?

3. What is meant by a "fair weather faith"?

4. What is the significance of saying "I **am** baptized"?

Discussion

1. Discuss a time when you "trusted" and were disappointed. Why do we find it difficult at times to trust?

2. How do you feel about making the sign of the cross over yourself when you get up in the morning and when you go to bed in the evening?

3. What does it mean to you that by baptism you have put on Christ like a suit of clothing?

4. Discuss what impact "wearing" Christ can have on a person.

Confession

Absolution

The Office Of The Keys

Confession

It is called an "inferiority complex." Almost everybody has it to some degree or the other. We demonstrate it by walking with our heads down, by bragging about how great we are, by feeling depressed, and so forth. What are some of the ways in which you sometimes feel inferior? Do you think that the fear of being rejected by others is also a symptom of this inferiority complex? Why do we all feel inferior? From where does this feeling come?

Lucy, of the Peanuts gang, has set up her roadside psychiatric stand: "The Doctor is IN. 5¢ please."

Charlie Brown (who really is "Everyman": he is us all) sits at her feet and complains: "Lucy, I feel inferior."

Lucy reassuringly responds: "Charlie Brown, you are inferior."

Yes, Charlie Brown is us all, and we all suffer from his problem. We feel inferior. Even the person who brags feels inferior. His (or her) loud mouth is only a cover-up for how he/she really feels. There is no escaping it; "inferiority" is a disease common to the entire human race. No one is exempt.

From where do these feelings of inferiority come? Why are we so plagued by them? Why do we all bear the marks of this disease, a disease which is more devastating than any other ever inflicted upon the human race?

According to a well-known and respected Christian psychiatrist, who is also very "in," Paul Tournier, inferiority traces its roots back to guilt. He states that guilt is the embryo (the egg) from which inferiority hatches. Because we are mortals, creatures rather than the creator, we not only are often confronted by a lot of things that we just can not do, we also all too often are confronted by the fact that there are a lot of things which we simply do badly, or which we should not have done at all.

Shame and guilt are related. When we feel guilty we feel ashamed. Usually when we feel ashamed it is because we feel guilty. Read Genesis 3:1-13. When Adam and Eve realized their guilt, how did they demonstrate their shame? How do little children sometimes demonstrate their shame when they know they are guilty? How do you demonstrate your shame when you feel guilty?

How do people sometimes try to hide their guilt? Their shame?

❖ ❖ ❖ ❖ ❖

It is inescapable, as Saint Paul himself bemoans, "The good that I would, I do not, and the evil that I would not, that I do … O, wretched man that I am" (Romans 7:19, 24 KJV).

That is the cry of Charlie Brown. That is the cry of everyone. That is the cry of our shared inferiority. That is our universal confession of guilt. That is the symptom of this awful disease that has inflicted every one of us.

What are we to do? What can we do with it, this disease?

In the *Small Catechism* Dr. Martin Luther addresses this problem in the section titled "Confession." First Luther asks the question, "What is Confession?" Then he gives this answer:

> *Confession has two parts. First, that we confess our sins and second, that we receive absolution, that is, forgiveness, from the pastor as from God Himself, not doubting, but firmly believing that by it our sins are forgiven before God in heaven.*

Then he asks: "What sins should we confess?"

> *Before God we should plead guilty of all sins, even those we are not aware of, as we do in the Lord's Prayer; but before the pastor we should confess only those sins which we know and feel in our hearts.*

❖ ❖ ❖ ❖ ❖
How is confession handled in your church? Is it a regular part of the worship service? If it is, do you appreciate that it is? What do you think about confessing to a pastor? Would you ever do it? What sins might you confess? What kinds of sins would you never want him nor anybody else to know about? Is hiding those sins part of what we call "guilt"? Do we hide our guilt because we are ashamed of it?
❖ ❖ ❖ ❖ ❖

Confessing one's sins, especially confessing particular sins, is not a popular activity these days. Confession has fallen upon hard times. Even in some churches where it once was mandatory, it is seldom seen or heard any more. In other congregations the people might still get on their knees on a Sunday morning for the unison saying of a General Confession. And then in some other churches confession of any sort seems to have disappeared altogether.

All of this might be because we live in a very private time. We prefer to let our private business be private. We don't care to talk about these things with others. Especially do we consider our relationship with God, and our religion, and our sins, to be private business and nobody else's. These things are personal matters, and we don't like to talk about them (especially our sins, those things which make us feel inferior) with anybody else. After all, why should we confess our sins to anybody? (Except, maybe, if we have hurt somebody or done something against another person; then maybe we should be honest enough and face up to it, and tell that person that we are sorry.)

The protest continues: Why should we tell others our sins? They hurt enough as it is. Besides, God is the one who is supposed to forgive. He really is the only one who has the right to forgive us for all the things we have done wrong. We don't need somebody in between who might not keep our secrets secret anyway.

❖ ❖ ❖ ❖ ❖
Some people might say that it is better to forget some sins and that the more that one focuses on them the worse one makes it for oneself. "Let sleeping dogs lie." What do you think about that? Also, if one knows that confessing some sin to someone else will only hurt that person (like confessing infidelity to a spouse, or a child confessing something which will bring shame to a parent), would it be better to remain silent about the sin? Can confessing ever do more damage than good?
❖ ❖ ❖ ❖ ❖

On the other hand, some observers have suggested that the reason why our society these days has such a great need for psychotherapists and psychoanalysts is because the guilt that once was handled by confession within the church no longer is cared for there, and consequently it is taken to the counselor's office, and for a rather handsome fee he or she does what the ministers of the church used to do for free.

❖ ❖ ❖ ❖ ❖
Do you think that because there is less confessing these days (for example to one another and to pastors) there is a greater need for psychiatrists and psychotherapists? Do you think that psychiatrists and psychotherapists or pastors are better equipped to hear confessions?
❖ ❖ ❖ ❖ ❖

Yes, there seems to be a great trend these days away from confessing one's sins in church to the pastor. Have you ever approached your pastor (to say nothing of doing it frequently) and said, "Pastor, please hear my confession"? In fact, when I speak to people who are not of the Lutheran Church about our confession of faith, I am sometimes asked, "Do you mean to say that you believe in confession?" They sound as if they think that "confession" is some kind of disease. I answer, "Of course we believe in confession." By that I don't mean just our confession of faith, for example, the Apostles' and the Nicene Creeds. ("I believe in God the Father Almighty ... and in Jesus Christ ... and in the Holy Spirit.") Nor do I mean simply saying, "I'm sorry," to a person whose feelings have been hurt or who has been treated somewhat discourteously, rudely, or whose feathers have been ruffled. Nor am I simply referring to the entire congregation assembled for worship on a Sunday morning beginning the service with a general confession of sins said by everybody together. No! When I respond with a "Yes" to the question, "Do you believe in Confession?" I am responding in the affirmative to what is called "private confession." Such a confessing is nothing less than hearing people tell me about their specific sins.

❖ ❖ ❖ ❖ ❖
Confessing that is done too easily doesn't get the job done. What is the biggest difference between saying, "I'm sorry," or the words of the congregation's confession on a Sunday morning, and "private" confession? Why is private confessing usually not an easy thing to do?
❖ ❖ ❖ ❖ ❖

That does not mean that because I have some insatiable prurient interest in people's misdeeds that I have invited them to tell me all the sordid details. I do not have a need to hear about their indiscretions so that I can sit/stand in judgment of them, although I think that some people fear and hesitate to tell their pastor or anyone else their sins, because they are sure that they will then be judged. There is the fear that the person who hears of their flaws will now think differently of them, will think less of them, and they feel badly enough already.

❖ ❖ ❖ ❖ ❖
Most of us suffer from a degree of inferiority already. Why would telling somebody our sins possibly make us feel even more inferior? When you hear of the sins of others, what is usually your reaction? One of forgiveness or one of judgment?
❖ ❖ ❖ ❖ ❖

Nevertheless, ministers, you see, are not supposed to sit in judgment of people. There is a plaque in my office which reads in part:

He (the pastor) will not be surprised at your sins, nor will he judge you in them, but he always invites you to share with him the wisdom and love of God, the knowledge of forgiveness of sins, and the saving grace of God.

Do you think that the church has a reputation of being forgiving of sinners or of being judgmental of sinners? How do you think your pastor would treat you, what would he think of you, if you confessed to him some private sin of which you were very ashamed? Do you think he would treat you the way the scribes and Pharisees treated the woman mentioned in John 8?

Ministers are not called primarily to be defenders and protectors of morals and values. They are not called to shake their fingers in contempt at all who sin. They are not a particular breed of men who are supposed to make people feel guilty. God knows we all feel guilt enough already. No wonder we also feel so inferior. Therefore, confessing to them is not supposed to awaken any more guilt so that there might be more condemnation. Instead, confession addresses guilt so that it can be healed.

Here is an example of just that. In the Gospel of Saint John, chapter 8, there is a story of the woman who was caught in the act of adultery. She was hauled before Jesus by the scribes and Pharisees, those very religious people of Jesus' day who knew all the law of Moses very well. They were good at pointing out if someone did something wrong.

Sometimes there is a great debate over whether we should forgive someone who has broken the rules or whether we should see to it that he or she is punished to the full extent of the law. If you were a judge, how would you handle such a situation? If you were (perhaps you are) a leader of the church, how would you handle such a situation? What does forgiveness do to justice?

They knew that Jesus was "easy" on sinners, that He preached a gospel of forgiveness. They also knew that the Law of Moses said that anyone caught in the act of adultery was to die by having stones thrown on top of them. So they brought this woman to Jesus to see how He would handle the case. If He agreed that she should die, then He was contradicting Himself, He who talked so much about forgiveness. However, if He suggested that she be set free, then He was going against the Law of Moses, and that would mean trouble for Him. Either way, they thought, they would make life miserable for Him whom they did not like anyway.

"Well, Jesus, what is your answer?"

Jesus did not have a quick answer for them. Instead we are told by John that He stalled a little bit, and then He began to trace in the dust with His finger. The question was not an easy one; neither would be the answer.

He finally looked up at them and said, "Let him who is without sin, without guilt, sit, stand, in judgment of others."

After Jesus had said that, His detractors left, not confessing their own guilt but still bearing that awful burden.

❖ ❖ ❖ ❖ ❖
According to the story in John 8 what did Jesus suggest that the accusers of the woman not do? What did He suggest that they do?
❖ ❖ ❖ ❖ ❖

For the woman, however, it was different. It was all out in the open now. And from there it was removed, as far as the East is from the West. That which had been red as crimson was now white as snow.

The woman had been set free: free from her past guilt and also free from being a slave to her sin again. She was set free from her inferiorities. Now she could walk through the streets of Jerusalem with her head held high for the first time in a long time.

That's what it means when we say that we believe in Confession!

❖ ❖ ❖ ❖ ❖
The real point of this story in John 8 is that the woman had a new lease on life. Because she confessed she was able to walk with her head high. Have you ever felt that way after having confessed? If so, why have you felt that way? What changed?
❖ ❖ ❖ ❖ ❖

Questions

1. What was the matter with Charlie Brown?

2. What is the common disease from which we all suffer?

3. From where does this disease come?

4. Why do we hesitate to confess our sins to anyone else?

5. What is one of the reasons why there is such a great need for psychiatrists these days?

6. Why should we confess our sins? What good will it do us?

7. When we are forgiven, from what are we set free?

Discussion

1. Do you think a reemphasis upon a personal exercise of confession would be helpful? Discuss how such an emphasis might take shape within the church.

2. Discuss your eagerness or hesitation to practice personal confession.

Absolution

❖ ❖ ❖ ❖ ❖
Attempts at "covering up" have gotten a lot of people into a lot of trouble. Recount persons (both public and private) who got themselves into a lot of trouble because of their attempts to cover up their mistakes. (Refer also again to Adam and Eve's attempt at covering up in Genesis 3.) What are the chances of being successful in "covering up"?
❖ ❖ ❖ ❖ ❖

A young couple, newly married and newly moved into an older home, decided that the house would need some remodeling. After securing a home improvement loan, they hired a carpenter to lower the ceilings and build bookcases, masons to put in a fireplace, and painters to paint. Then they ran low on money. Consequently, the young husband decided that he would have to put in the carpeting himself. A trip to the library provided him with the necessary books to show him how to do it. After he had read them and felt that he was ready, he measured and calculated, bought the necessary tools, and ordered the carpeting. Early on a Saturday morning he started. He cleared out the furniture, carefully laid down the padding, unrolled and stretched out the carpeting, and then carefully tacked it down. Several exhausting hours later, he was finished. Standing up to admire his work, he reached into his pocket for a cigarette. The pocket was empty. He thought he remembered something slipping out of his pocket earlier. He looked around the newly laid carpet and there, several feet from one end, he noticed a lump. "Oh, no," he groaned. He walked over to the spot and said to himself, "There's no way that I'm going to tear it all up and start over again." So he lifted his foot and brought it down hard, squashing the object. Then he said, "I'll put the sofa over it. No one will ever know." Satisfied, he went into the kitchen and announced to his wife, "Honey, it's done." Then continuing almost without thinking and certainly forgetting about the lump under the rug he asked, "Oh, by the way, have you seen my cigarettes?" "Sure," she replied. "They're right over here on the windowsill where you left them. And, by the way, have you seen the parakeet?"

It seems, doesn't it, that in one way or the other we all try so hard to cover up our mistakes. And our sins. Yet just as often they seem to betray us, and we realize that the cover-up doesn't work. So did the Tell-Tale Heart cry out from beneath Edgar Allen Poe's hardwood floor. So also was it with Shakespeare's Lady Macbeth. Whenever another dead body turned up in Inverness Castle she protested, "I didn't do it. I didn't do it." Yet her guilty conscience struck her so hard that late at night she wandered through the halls of the castle in nightmarish trances trying to wash her hands clean of the imaginary blood which stained them. She pleaded as she looked at them, "Out, damned spot; out, I say." But it was to no avail. It was her guilty conscience which she tried to hide from others which finally betrayed her before all. So also was the case with the "Tell-all Heart" in Poe's short story mystery.

In addition to being embarrassed by what we have done, do you think that one of the main reasons people are hesitant to confess is because they are not sure that they will be forgiven? Can you think of anyone (perhaps even yourself) who after confessing was not forgiven, and in fact, got into even more difficulty because of the confession? Do you think there is some benefit in confessing even when forgiveness is not pronounced? Does the confessing do the confessor good nevertheless?

❖ ❖ ❖ ❖ ❖

The question is, "Why do we try so hard to hide our sins? Is it because confessing is so hard to do? Is it because we are so ashamed and embarrassed? Or is it that we are not sure that we will be forgiven? Perhaps this latter answer is the case. Certainly confessing is a hard business. Certainly we wish not everybody to know our secret faults. But to be sure of being forgiven: that is difficult, indeed.

Perhaps it is because we find it so hard to be forgiving that we also find it so hard to be sure of being forgiven. Therefore, the game of hiding our sins goes on. We think that we can mask our guilty consciences.

The trouble with confessing is not just with our hesitation to confess. The problem often is with the reluctance of those who hear the confession to offer forgiveness. What might be some circumstances in which you would hold back on offering forgiveness? What are some things that people do that you just would not be able to forgive? Do you think that there are any sins so great that God would not forgive? Under what circumstances would God not forgive?

❖ ❖ ❖ ❖ ❖

It is not that we are totally unforgiving. There is at least a little bit of mercy in all of our hearts. If someone is really sincere about asking for forgiveness, and the sin is not too great, we probably would bring ourselves around to forgive them — at least a few times. Perhaps seven is enough. That is what the disciples thought. After all, there have to be limits. "No! No!" Jesus says. Seven times is not enough. "You better make it seven times seventy." Forgiveness must be without limits.

Can you think of anything for which there are no limits? Is even space limitless? We seem to live in a world in which there are limits for everything. Do you think there ought to be limits placed on the forgiveness extended to "repeat offenders"? Do you think that forgiveness can also lead to "enabling" some people to continue with their negative and hurtful behavior? Address the issues of forgiving and enabling. Does the one foster the other? How can one be forgiving and yet not enabling?

A story about forgiveness without limits which Jesus told, and which is one of my favorite Bible stories, is the one we sometimes call the "Parable of the Prodigal Son" (Luke 15). I like to call it the "Parable of the Father of Prodigals." I say that because I think that the real emphasis in the story is not on the behavior of the son, as bad as it is, but on the graciousness of the father which is contrasted by the unforgiving heart of the elder son.

As you read the story of the Prodigal Son (the Father of Prodigals) either from Luke 15 or here, place yourself into the story. Do you see yourself as the younger son? Do you ever see yourself as the elder brother? Do you ever see yourself as the Father?

Certainly the behavior of the younger son is despicable. He couldn't even wait until his father was dead. And when his father didn't die soon enough to suit him, he demanded, "Give me my share of the inheritance now; I can't wait any longer. I must run with my friends." The good father knew that he must let his son go. He must let him go squander his money, make a fool of himself, and, if need be, even slop the pigs.

When this foolish younger son hit bottom, he came to his senses. He returned home, repented, and confessed to his father what shame he had brought both upon himself and upon the family. He felt so badly about what he had done that he didn't even ask for full forgiveness. He didn't think that he deserved it. He was willing to live as a hired servant of his father. He was content to live in the bunkhouse. The big house, he was sure, would not have him back.

❖ ❖ ❖ ❖ ❖
This is a story about a "homecoming." What is the home? What makes the homecoming possible? What are some characteristics of a joyful homecoming? Have you ever gone to a homecoming? Why are homecomings important?
❖ ❖ ❖ ❖ ❖

His father, however, would have none of that. His son had come home! He ran out to meet him. He hugged him. He kissed him. He threw his arms around him and embraced him. His son had come home!

The embracing of this son is what forgiveness is all about. This is the heart of the matter. To forgive means that you are willing to throw your arms around someone again, someone who has in some way hurt you. It means that you are willing to let that person get close to you again.

Let's look at that Father of Prodigals. He did not take his son back on condition (on condition that he behave himself, or that he pay back what he had lost, or that he serve some time on probation). No! Instead, unconditionally he welcomed him back, after which he began to prepare a banquet (a real celebration, a feast at which would be served the finest fare, and to which would be invited everyone who would come).

❖ ❖ ❖ ❖ ❖
Can we ever reconcile fairness with forgiveness? If God was fair with us, how much forgiveness would we get? If we were fair with each other, how much forgiveness would we give? What happens to justice when there is too much forgiveness? When grace is cheap what can be the serious consequences?
❖ ❖ ❖ ❖ ❖

The eldest son, on the other hand, the one who had played it straight all those years, bristled. This just wasn't fair. But then forgiveness is not about fairness. We can all be glad for that. For if we received what was fair, if we received what we deserved, ours would be a sorry lot, indeed.

You see the real problem in this story is not with the younger son but with the older one. He resented that his father took the younger one back. (He even refused to call him his brother.) So he protested. He boycotted the dinner. He was certain that people who do wrong must be made to pay.

I am afraid that we often feel the same way. In addition we don't want to hand out forgiveness too quickly, because the person who did wrong once just might do wrong twice. Can we really trust people who have bad records? Forgiveness that comes too easily might simply encourage more bad behavior.

Is it not true that as people of the church we also must stand for that which is right? We must defend good standards and values. If forgiveness is made too easy that will only encourage people to sin all the more. Yes, grace must not be made cheap, or the church will lose its credibility. It will run the risk of becoming wishy-washy. Forgiveness must be dealt out carefully and maybe even a big stingily.

Nevertheless, in spite of saying all of that: "Behold the Father of Prodigals." We know who that is, don't we? Yes, the Father of Prodigals is God Himself.

Think of it: If God were to put us on trial for all of our sins, if He were to question the honesty of our confessions, I think that He would keep us up all night asking questions, investigating our sincerity.

But that is not the way God operates. Therefore, at the end of each day, as I put my head on my pillow, I ask God to forgive me, and I know that He does. Therefore, I am able to go to sleep immediately. God does not keep me up all night grilling me and cross-examining me and questioning my sincerity. He simply forgives me. Without question he removes my guilt as far as from the East is from the West. He turns that which was red like crimson into that which is as white as snow. Such a Father I, as a prodigal son, have.

Do you ever wonder if you are fully forgiven? Is there anything you can do to make sure that you are fully forgiven? If you are not fully forgiven, what are the consequences? Can you ever be only partially forgiven by God, or must it be an "all or nothing" deal?

❖ ❖ ❖ ❖ ❖

You see, we confess not so that we can be sentenced and condemned. We confess so that we can be set free, so that we can be absolved. That's what forgiveness is. It is being set free.

Imagine this: The scene is that of a courtroom. The jury has just returned from its deliberations. The foreman of the jury stands before the judge and says, "We the jury find the defendant guilty as charged ... but forgiven." Absolved!

How can that be? It is that way for us because God, who is a just God, directed all His judgment upon His Son, Jesus, who as our Savior hung upon the cross in our stead. Yes, forgiveness and grace are not cheap. They have come at great cost. They cost the Son of God His very life! That is what makes forgiveness doubly precious and dear to us.

How much sense does it make to you that even though you are guilty, God declares you forgiven, and that the consequences for your sins are placed upon the shoulders of Jesus as He hung upon the cross? Does that satisfy the demands of justice? Does that have any impact on the problem of enabling?

❖ ❖ ❖ ❖ ❖

God is a good and a gracious God. He binds up the brokenhearted. He heals the wounded. He strengthens the knees of the weak. That is what forgiveness does for those who confess, for those who know how to turn to the Father of Prodigals — the Father of the prodigal sons and daughters which we all are.

What do you think is the most significant, the most meaningful, story in the Bible? Why is it so important? Why do you feel that way? Do you think the parable of the Father of Prodigals is that story or similar to that story?

❖ ❖ ❖ ❖ ❖

Remember, confession has two parts: one, that we confess our sins; and two, that we receive forgiveness, that we are absolved. We can be sure that we receive forgiveness, because the One who does the forgiving is none other than the Father of Prodigals, God Himself, who saw to it that the price that needed to be paid for our sins was offered by none other than His dear Son, Jesus, our Lord.

Questions

1. What did the story about the man laying carpet in the house tell us about trying to cover up our sins?

2. What do "guilty" consciences sooner or later do?

3. What are the two reasons why confessing is hard to do?

4. How often can we be sure we are forgiven? How often should we forgive?

5. Why might the "Parable of the Prodigal Son" be renamed the "Parable of the Father of Prodigals"?

6. What was wrong with the elder son?

7. Even though we might be guilty, what does God declare us to be?

8. Why is forgiveness not cheap when it comes from God?

Discussion

1. Discuss the difference between being sure that you are forgiven and the gnawing need to make amends for what you have done wrong.

2. Do you see yourself in the parable of "The Father of Prodigals"? If so, discuss how and in what way. For example, do you find yourself identifying with the father, with the younger son, with the elder son, or with anyone else for that matter?

The Office Of The Keys

❖ ❖ ❖ ❖ ❖
What are some of the reasons why peace is often lacking in our families? In your own family, why are there sometimes tensions? The church is also often referred to as a family. Why does the church also sometimes have tensions among its members? What are some of the tensions at your church? Who caused them? How do you think they can be reduced if not eliminated altogether?
❖ ❖ ❖ ❖ ❖

Keeping peace in the family — that is what the Office of the Keys is all about.

Yes, peace in the family — what a blessing it is. However, the family to which I am now referring is not so much the family at home as it is the family at church, the church family, the Christian community. It, this family, longs for peace. It dreams of peace.

Yet within the church there often seems to be so little of that precious peace. The members of the church family fight with one another just as do members of any other family. In this respect it is not much different than any other organization of people.

However, in another respect, the church is altogether different. That is because to the family of the church God has given a special gift; we call it "The Office of the Keys."

When we refer to the Office of the Keys, we obviously don't mean the keys to the office, the church office. Well, then, just what is the Office of the Keys? For the answer to that question we once again turn to Dr. Martin Luther's *Small Catechism.*

The Office of the Keys is that special authority which Christ has given to His church on earth to forgive the sins of repentant sinners, but to withhold forgiveness from the unrepentant as long as they do not repent.

Where is this written?

This is what Saint John the Evangelist writes in chapter twenty: The Lord Jesus breathed on His disciples and said, "Receive the Holy Spirit. If you forgive anyone his sins, they are forgiven; if you do not forgive them, they are not forgiven." — John 20:22-23

Words have tremendous power. They can hurt or they can heal. They can destroy or they can build up. Think of the power they have when somebody says, "I hate you," and also of the power they have when somebody says, "I love you." The power of words also rests with the authority that is behind them. Compare the difference between saying something (especially making promises) without authority with saying something because you have authority. What might be some of those situations? What difference does it make when we forgive somebody by the authority that comes from God? To whom has God given the authority to forgive? (Refer to John 20:22-23.) Who are the disciples referred to in this Bible passage? Are there disciples around today? Who might they be?

There is a rather interesting history behind this idea of the Office of the Keys. In early times, way, way back, during the first few centuries of the Christian church's life, Christians were often subject to a lot of persecution. There was a lot of pressure put upon them to deny the faith. Under the threat of death — threatened to be burned at the stake or thrown to the lions and so forth — a lot of people cracked under the pressure. In order to save their own necks, they renounced their faith, Christianity. And if that was not bad enough, they were often forced to give the names of other Christians to those who were doing the persecuting. Consequently, the ranks of the church were often raided. Indeed, a lot of folks lost their lives, all because some had given in to the pressure, had betrayed the faith, and had purchased their own safety at the expense of someone else's life.

What was the church to do with those persons who, once the heat was off, wanted back in? Should they welcome them with open arms in spite of the horrible and traitorous things they had done? Or should they be denied God's grace? Should they be cut off from the Word and the Sacraments?

What to do with "turncoats" (traitors) is a difficult question. Have you ever met a "traitor"? What was the circumstance? How did you feel about the traitor? Would you forgive a traitor? Would you be willing to trust a traitor? What is the foundation upon which trust is built? Are there any circumstances in which you might be a traitor yourself? Can you justify and excuse traitorous behavior? Is it true, "Once a traitor, always a traitor"?

❖ ❖ ❖ ❖ ❖

The question was asked: "If we let these people back in, can we ever trust them again, or once back in will they only reveal the names of more Christians to our persecutors? Will these traitors come back into the church as spies, as moles?"

Obviously, congregations were reluctant to let back in such scoundrels. After all, wasn't a denial of the faith a sin against the Holy Ghost? Was there ever forgiveness for such a terrible thing? Wasn't this the unpardonable sin?

It is said that the unforgivable sin is the sin against the Holy Ghost. That sin is identifiable as "denying the faith." Can someone who denies the faith ever repent and ask for forgiveness? When is the sin against the Holy Ghost the unforgivable sin?

❖ ❖ ❖ ❖ ❖

So it was that many of those Christians who had not denied the faith concluded that these persons who had should under no circumstances be allowed back into the fellowship of believers. There simply was no forgiveness for them. They could not be trusted. To let them back in would only be foolish. It would be an invitation to trouble.

Yet, there were such incidents as that with Simon Peter that had to be reckoned with. Do you remember how it was on that night when Jesus was betrayed by Judas? Peter, standing in the courtyard of the high priest, denied knowing Jesus. Three times he denied his Lord! He acted like a traitor, and he did it all in order to save his own neck. He was afraid that he was also going to be arrested. Now the question was: Could Peter ever be trusted again?

Of course he was to be trusted. He eventually even became one of the most significant and influential leaders in the early church. To him Jesus Himself said, "You are Peter, and to you I will give the keys to the Kingdom of Heaven."

❖ ❖ ❖ ❖ ❖
Was Peter's sin of denying Jesus a sin against the Holy Ghost? What were the circumstances behind Peter denying Jesus? What would you have done if you had been in his shoes?
❖ ❖ ❖ ❖ ❖

I think that incident recorded in Matthew 16 (Jesus committing to Peter the Keys of Heaven, the very keys to forgiveness) had something to do with the attitude of the church toward the turncoats who had repented. They, if they publicly confessed their sin of denying the faith and showed sincerity in their confession, were to be forgiven. They were to be restored as members of the family of faith.

❖ ❖ ❖ ❖ ❖
Refer to Matthew 16:13-19. Compare that to Matthew 26:69-75. Do you think that Matthew deliberately included these two events so that we could compare them and see them side by side? When you compare these two sections of Scripture, what do they say to you?
❖ ❖ ❖ ❖ ❖

In situations like that we can envision the exercise of the Office of the Keys as a reopening to them of the gates of heaven. Forgiveness unlocked the doors that had kept them from the Word and the Sacraments. Yes, even traitors could be welcomed back into where grace and mercy abounded.

As the years went on, however, not so many Christians were persecuted because of their faith. Christianity, in fact, eventually became the official religion of the Roman Empire. Thus, the Office of the Keys then had to take on a different dimension. For example, during the Middle Ages there developed the practice of confessing one's sins to a priest, a minister, especially if a person's conscience was burdened with a lot of guilt.

❖ ❖ ❖ ❖ ❖
Do you think it is necessary to confess your sins to a pastor? Do you think it is good to confess your sins to a pastor? Do you think it is wise to confess your sins to another person (other than a pastor)? Would that other person have the right, power, authority to forgive you your sins? To whom do you think Galatians 6:2 is addressed? Are people today included? Are you included?
❖ ❖ ❖ ❖ ❖

Guilt, associated with unforgivable sins, is a terrible burden to carry around. Sins unforgiven not only weigh heavily upon one's spirit, but they also bar the gates of heaven. You see, it is only forgiveness which opens heaven's gates wide. And that's the point! To tell others, other Christians, what it is that is burdening one's conscience so that they can speak to the troubled person the words of God's grace and forgiveness, is what sets free. Troubled consciences need to hear those words.

Think of Galatians 6:2: "Bear one another's burdens and so fulfill the law of Christ." That means, "Carry away the burden of the guilt of the sins of others. Carry that burden far, far away." That is what forgiveness is all about.

Therefore, to those who confess Christ as Lord and Savior, as did Peter at Caesarea Philippi (Matthew 16), there is given the ministry of the Office of the Keys. Yes! They can open the gates of heaven to and for troubled consciences.

❖ ❖ ❖ ❖ ❖
According to Matthew 16, who has the right to forgive sins?
❖ ❖ ❖ ❖ ❖

In order to make sure that this ministry of forgiveness continues, the church has seen fit to call pastors. Pastors are called by Christian congregations so that those who confess their sins might hear the words of forgiveness spoken every week. There are other things that pastors also do, but declaring the forgiveness of sins is among the most important. In order to remind them of this special task, they wear what is called a "stole." A stole is really a yoke; it binds the pastor to God as a minister of the Gospel, and it binds him to the congregation he serves, reminding him to be ready at all times and under all circumstances to declare forgiveness to all those who repent. The opposite is also true. Pastors are to declare that there is no forgiveness to those who do not repent.

❖ ❖ ❖ ❖ ❖
Do you think that the Church and its ministry would survive without pastors? What qualifications should pastors have before they serve a congregation? Who should be allowed to be a pastor? From where do pastors get the authority to do what they do? Should pastors be "out front" leading the congregations they serve, or should they merely do what they are told to do?
❖ ❖ ❖ ❖ ❖

I remember a lady who was intending to join the congregation which I was serving at the time saying to me, "Reverend, I have no trouble in joining your church, except that I can't quite accept it when at the beginning of the service after the confession of sins, you say 'I, by virtue of my office, as a called and ordained servant of the Word ... forgive you all your sins.' I thought that only God has the right to forgive sins like that."

Well, her first problem was in addressing me as "Reverend." Yes, an ordained clergyman, "Reverend" is a title by which, in formal situations, I am addressed. But as a minister, as her servant, I am her pastor. A pastor is one who serves; he is not one who rules. In addition, I don't glide a few inches above the ground. I get dust on my shoes as does everybody else. I am not a "high and mighty Reverend." I do not have special powers. All I have is a special assignment — a job to be done in the service of others. So, I believe, all pastors must always come to their congregations from down below and not from above, from on high.

Pastors are supposed to declare the forgiveness of sins. Can you think of situations when pastors should declare that sins are not forgiven? How would you feel if a pastor refused to forgive you your sin(s)? What might be a circumstance in which that might happen? If a pastor says to somebody that his or her sin(s) is not forgiven, what do you think that pastor should also do? (Refer to Matthew 18:15-22.) What if a pastor has a difference of opinion with the majority of the congregation that "called" him to be their pastor? What might be such a situation? How should it be handled?

This good lady's second problem was that she called it "my" church. No church of which I have ever been pastor was "my" church. I have never been the boss of any congregation. Instead, as a servant, I must speak the words of God's forgiveness whenever it is asked for. I can not hold it back for my own reasons.

In the final analysis, from where comes the authority to forgive sins? To whom has that authority been given? How important is the forgiveness of sins to you? How essential do you think it is to the life of a congregation?

Finally, remember also that the forgiveness that the pastor proclaims is also not to be regarded as a pill which he dispenses and which may also be withheld from those whom he might not want to have it. Forgiveness is not to be granted only to those who are in his favor. Remember, the Office of the Keys does not belong to any one person. Rather, it has been entrusted to the whole church, the church which says, "We need to hear the Word of God's forgiveness spoken in our midst each week." Therefore, the church, individual churches, congregations, call pastors so that they can be sure that they will hear the Word of forgiveness spoken as from God Himself each and every week. It is the most important Word to be spoken all week.

❖ ❖ ❖ ❖ ❖

If a husband and wife say to each other, "I love you," on the day that they are married, do they ever need to say those words to each other again? Do you think that there is a relationship between saying those words repeatedly and hearing words of forgiveness repeatedly? How important is it to you to hear words of forgiveness? Do you think that saying those words to the members of a congregation is a pastor's most important responsibility?

❖ ❖ ❖ ❖ ❖

The Office of the Keys is the ministry of the Word of God declaring forgiveness to those who seek it and declaring that where it is not sought there is no forgiveness. To make sure that happens, congregations call pastors.

Questions

1. Why did some early Christians sometimes deny the faith?

2. What did they sometimes do under pressure?

3. Why did they want back in the church?

4. Who betrayed Jesus?

5. Who denied Jesus three times?

6. Who should be let back into the church? What must they first do?

7. Who needs to hear words of forgiveness?

8. Why does the pastor wear a stole?

9. What is the most important thing a pastor does?

10. What is a pastor?

11. What does it mean for a pastor to be "called"?

Discussion

1. The shape of church membership is often colored and defined by the spirit of the times. Discuss ways in which church membership is different today than fifty years ago, 100 years ago, and so forth.

2. What is expected of pastors also changes with the times. What expectations would you consider to be important in these times?

Holy Communion — The Sacrament Of The Altar

Holy Communion — The Sacrament Of The Altar: Part One

❖ ❖ ❖ ❖ ❖
What are the nine parts of speech (nine kinds of words) in the English language? What is the function of each? Words (all kinds) are important, because with them we think. Words make the connection between what IS and what we KNOW. A wise man once said, "You don't know what you can't say." Do you think that is true? Have you ever discovered that you came to know something when you found the words with which to express yourself?
❖ ❖ ❖ ❖ ❖

What is a preposition?

In the English language a preposition is a word which shows a relationship between a substantive (that's a noun or pronoun) and a verb, an adjective, or another substantive. A preposition is, for example: *to, at, by, above, in, with,* or *under*.

Why did I ask, "What is a preposition?" and why did I then give the answer to that question? This certainly isn't a book on grammar, on the proper use of words. But it is a book of words by a Lutheran pastor about another book of words, the *Small Catechism,* written by the first Lutheran pastor, Dr. Martin Luther. In his book Dr. Luther presented a short explanation of the chief parts of the Christian faith. That explanation brings us now to his and our discussion of the Sacrament of the Altar, or Holy Communion. Soon you shall see that prepositions are a very important part of our endeavor to understand just what is Holy Communion.

In order for that to happen we must go all the way back to the night when Jesus instituted this action. It was at the time of Passover almost 2,000 years ago. We call that night when Jesus sat with his disciples around the table in the Upper Room "Maundy Thursday." It was the same night in which Jesus was betrayed by Judas Iscariot. That was the night in which Jesus was arrested. It was the night before He was crucified. It was the night which, along with Christmas Eve, is the most holy of all nights for Christians.

❖ ❖ ❖ ❖ ❖

Reconstruct the events of Holy Week beginning with Palm Sunday and ending with Easter. What happened on each day? (Refer to Matthew 21-28, Mark 11-16, and Luke 19-24.)

❖ ❖ ❖ ❖ ❖

Jesus was about to observe the Festival of the Passover with his disciples. Back in Bible times, and even today in many Jewish homes, whenever the Passover is to be celebrated the entire family gathers around the table set with all sorts of good things to eat. Once the family is assembled there, it is customary for the youngest child present to ask the father of the family this question: "Why is this night special above all other nights?"

Reconstruct the event of the original Passover. (Refer to Exodus 12.) How important do you think is the connection between the sacrifice of the lambs' blood at the time of the Exodus and the sacrifice of Christ's (the Lamb of God) blood on Calvary? The one sacrifice led to a certain kind of freedom. What was it? The other sacrifice led to another kind of freedom. What is it?

Meals seem to have an important place in celebrations. What are some significant celebrations which include meals? Why do you think sitting around tables and eating is such an important part of celebrations? What is the effect when the food and drink are of an inferior quality? Along with the food and drink, what is an important ingredient of mealtime (including, of course, meals which are part of celebrations)?

❖ ❖ ❖ ❖ ❖

The father of the family then answers by telling the story of the first Passover. This story tells of the blood of the lamb being smeared on the door frames of the homes of the ancient Israelites who were slaves in Egypt. That was over 3,000 years ago. The story also tells of how an angel of death passing through the land and claiming the firstborn of each family "passed over" the homes which had the blood of the lamb over the door. This story concludes with Moses leading the Children of Israel out of their Egyptian slavery into freedom, the freedom of the Promised Land.

After the story has been told, the youngest child asks a second question: "What difference does this make? What's so important about this story for today?"

A reciting of events from the past is also an important ingredient for celebrations. Why do you think that is so? Can you remember celebration events where remembering the past was included? Can you remember celebration events where remembering was not included? Contrast the two kinds of celebrations. Was one a better party than the other? If so, why? Why is it that the past is so important to the present? Why also is the future so important to the present?

❖ ❖ ❖ ❖ ❖

Again the father gives the answer, reminding the members of the family that it is important to remember the mighty acts of God.

Then follows the third question: "Why do we still observe this feast today?" Again the father speaks, this time emphasizing the fact that even as God remembered His people of old, He remembers them today.

Finally the fourth question is asked: "Why do we eat lamb, unleavened bread, and bitter herbs?" The father then explains the symbolic quality and meaning of this special menu.

So it was that each time that the family celebrated the Festival of the Passover, all present were reminded of "what" they were doing and "why" they were doing it. A question was asked and an answer was given.

In Jewish families when the Passover is being celebrated, four questions are asked focusing on what is happening and why it is happening. Do you think that it is something more than a mere coincidence that in his *Small Catechism* Martin Luther asks and answers four questions which focus on what is happening and why it is happening? Do you think he is making a conscious connection between Holy Communion and the Passover?

In our New Testament churches our coming to the altar to receive the Lord's supper (Holy Communion) is in some ways like the Jewish people participating in the Festival of the Passover meal. Therefore, it is also important for us to know and to understand "what" we are doing and "why" we are doing it. For that reason Dr. Luther, the sixteenth century reformer, also included in the *Small Catechism* four questions, all of which focus our attention on this sacrament.

The first question is: "What is the Sacrament of the Altar?" His answer to that question is:

It is the true body and blood of our Lord Jesus Christ under the bread and wine, instituted by Christ Himself for us Christians to eat and to drink.

Then he asks: "Where is this written?" And he gives the answer:

The holy Evangelists Matthew, Mark, Luke, and Saint Paul write:
Our Lord Jesus Christ, on the night when He was betrayed, took bread, and when He had given thanks, He broke it and gave it to the disciples and said: "Take, eat; this is My body, which is given for you. This do in remembrance of Me."
In the same way also He took the cup after supper, and when He had given thanks, He gave it to them, saying, "Drink of it, all of you; this cup is the new testament in My blood, which is shed for you for the forgiveness of sins. This do, as often as you drink it, in remembrance of Me."

So, there you have it: the question and the answer.

Martin Luther said that the Sacrament of Holy Communion IS the true body and blood of our Lord Jesus. He emphasized that the bread and the wine ARE our Lord's body and blood; they are not just symbols, representations, of that. That understanding hinges on the little yet most powerful word in the English language — the most powerful word in the Greek or Hebrew languages, indeed, the most powerful word in any and every language — the verb "to be" which equals IS.

Did not Jesus say, "This is My body"?

Did not Jesus say, "This is My blood"?

No doubt about it!

❖ ❖ ❖ ❖ ❖

The word "is" is a verb, one of the parts of speech. How is what "is" means different than something which is a symbol or something which represents something else?

The word "is" is probably the only word which really is what it is. Everything else is a symbol. Interestingly enough, in the Old Testament when God identified Himself to Moses, He called Himself by the verb "is" (in the Hebrew language, "Yahweh"). If anything is, God is. Does this help you to understand the presence of the Body and Blood of Christ in the Sacrament of Holy Communion: that the bread is His Body and that the wine is His Blood?

❖ ❖ ❖ ❖ ❖

The verb "to be," the verb "is," you see, stands for that which is, that which has being, that which exists. Everything else is merely imagination, a dream, a fantasy. But what is, IS. It is for real.

However, you might say, "All I see in Holy Communion is bread and wine. How can that possibly be the body and blood of Jesus Himself?"

The mystery of Christ's Body and Blood being present in Holy Communion has always challenged the human imagination. Therefore, since it is hard to understand how something can be two things at the same time, some have said that the bread and wine are changed into Body and Blood, while others have said that the bread and wine symbolized the Body and Blood. What do you think?
❖ ❖ ❖ ❖ ❖

This is where those prepositions come in. They will help us to understand. Luther explained that the body and blood of Jesus are ours "in, with, and under" the bread and the wine.

As mentioned earlier, a preposition is a word which shows a relationship. It connects two or more things together. So we say that in Holy Communion the bread and the wine and the body and the blood of Jesus are connected. They stand in relationship to each other. When you have the one you have the other.

To put it another way, let's speak of the visible elements in Holy Communion: the bread and the wine. They taste like bread and wine. They look like bread and wine. They must be bread and wine. How is it possible then that we say that here is the real body and blood of Jesus? How can we say that here He is really present when what we have before us is bread and wine?

We can say that for one reason and one reason only. We can say that because Jesus said it, because His word promises it. After all, since it was His very word which also created the entire universe (all that there is), His word is also able to make happen in the Sacrament what He says happens. Our human reason might not know how that is possible. But the prepositions "in, with, and under" help us to at least understand in part. They help us to understand that in Holy Communion, by means of that bread and wine, our Lord gets in touch with us.

Since God's Word is the most powerful thing in the entire universe and beyond (it called what is into being out of nothing), do you think it is powerful enough to work a miracle here, the miracle of Christ's Body and Blood being present "in, with, and under" the bread and wine? Do the prepositions "in, with, and under" help you to understand the relationship between the bread and wine and the Body and Blood?
❖ ❖ ❖ ❖ ❖

Do you remember the story about Helen Keller and Anne Sullivan? Helen Keller, when only about one-and-one-half years old, contracted a fever which left her blind and deaf for life. From that moment on she entered a private world. No one could communicate with her. She was in isolation from the rest of the human race. No one could talk to her. She could talk to no one.

❖ ❖ ❖ ❖ ❖

Can you imagine what it would be like not to have the use of the senses of sight and sound? Would you feel cut off from the rest of the world if you did not have the use of your eyes and ears?

❖ ❖ ❖ ❖ ❖

To assist them in raising Helen, her parents found Anne Sullivan, who became not only Helen's teacher, but also her friend. Anne Sullivan helped Helen to see by touching — flowers, animals, furniture. One day at the outside water pump, Helen began to splash in the water with her hands. She suddenly said, "Wah-wah." She had spoken this "word" years before, before her illness, when she was only one-and-one-half years old. Anne Sullivan immediately began to spell out the word "water" on the hand of Helen. That opened up a whole new world for her. Together the two ladies worked on Helen communicating with others. It was all done by touch — spelling things out on the palm of her hand. It was by the sense of touch that the barriers between Helen Keller and the rest of the people of the world came tumbling down.

❖ ❖ ❖ ❖ ❖

The sense of touch is an important one. Compare and contrast a hug with a hit (two kinds of touches). What does a hit do to two people? What does a hug do to two people? Since there is quite a distance between us and God, does this idea of God being in touch with us in Holy Communion help you to understand and appreciate the value of this Sacrament?

❖ ❖ ❖ ❖ ❖

There are communication barriers between God and us. One can say that we are from two different worlds. But in Holy Communion contact is made. God gets in touch with us by means of this Sacrament, and the barriers start to come tumbling down. Yes, here, indeed, we are in touch with Jesus. "Here," He says, "is My body for you. Here is My blood for you. Here I AM for you. I am as real as the bread you eat and the wine you drink." Here is the real presence of Jesus, made possible by the power of His word.

Now then, "What is the Sacrament of the Altar?" It is the real presence of Jesus in, with, and under the bread and wine for us. It is God being in touch with us.

Questions

1. Why are prepositions so useful in helping us to understand the relationship between the bread and the wine and the body and the blood of Jesus in the Sacrament of the Altar?

2. What makes it possible for the body and the blood of Jesus to be present in the Sacrament of Holy Communion for us?

3. How did Anne Sullivan help Helen Keller communicate?

Discussion

1. Review the four questions and answers asked and given whenever the Passover is celebrated, and compare them with the four questions Martin Luther asks in the *Small Catechism* with regard to Holy Communion.

2. Discuss how two worlds get in touch in Holy Communion.

Holy Communion — The Sacrament Of The Altar: Part Two

Why are you reading this book, this chapter? Why are you doing what you are doing right now? Is there a reason behind what you are doing? Are you doing it by your own choice, or are you doing it because you are being forced to do it? How do you feel about doing something when you don't know why you are doing it? Is that worse than doing something you are being forced to do?

Picture in your mind's eye kneeling in front of the altar in your church. It is there, at the altar, that Christians come to eat and drink the bread and wine of Holy Communion. Why?

That question "Why?" is a very important question, because, you see, we really don't do much for which there is no reason. There must be a purpose, a reason, behind everything that we do.

Sometimes, however, the reason why we do something might not be our own reason. There are times when we find that we are doing something because someone else is making us do it. Sometimes we are pressured into doing things. We might even not like what we are doing. But there is still a reason behind it. Nobody builds roads that go nowhere. Yes, there must be a reason for every bit of our behavior.

Therefore, I now ask, "Why go to Communion? Why eat the bread and drink the wine of the Sacrament of the Altar?" There must be a reason.

Do you think people who participate in Holy Communion are always aware of why they are doing so? What might be various reasons why people go to the altar to receive Communion? What leads you to answer the way you have?

In order to help us with this question we once again turn to Dr. Martin Luther's *Small Catechism*. In the section on Holy Communion he asks a second question (after the first one, "What is the Sacrament of the Altar?"): "For what purpose do we receive Holy Communion?" or "What is the benefit of this eating and drinking?" Here, from the *Catechism,* is the answer:

> *These words, "Given and shed for you for the forgiveness of sins," show us that in the Sacrament forgiveness of sins, life, and salvation are given us through these words. For where there is forgiveness of sins, there is also life and salvation.*

Every cell in our bodies does whatever it can to stay alive. What are some of the things we do so that we might stay alive? How successful do you think you will be in keeping yourself alive? For how long? Why will you ultimately be faced by death? Refer to Romans 6:23. Why do all people eventually die? In the face of death, what is our one hope?

We eat so that we might live. We drink so that we might live. We cannot live very long without food or drink. Even though we sometimes like to eat and drink because of the taste, ultimately we do it because otherwise we would die. Death haunts us all, and we all do the best we can to put off "the Grim Reaper." We try to dodge him for as long as we can. Eating properly is a highly recommended way to stay healthy and alive. There simply is no substitute for a good diet.

When receiving the Sacrament of the Altar Christians also eat and drink so that they might live. But the life of which I am now speaking is something more than just that which is measured in terms of years and decades — the passage of time. The life of which I am speaking has an eternal dimension to it. The big problem, however, is that it is not ours by nature. In fact, none of us has a right to it. Instead, just the opposite is true. As one man once said, "None of us is going to get out of here alive." We are all going to die. We are all mortal. Our life span has both a beginning and an end. We all have a problem.

Why do you think that death is not the end for people? Or do we just wish that it is not the end?

We have that problem because of what happened in the Garden of Eden. Apparently, it did not take very long for Adam and Eve, the first two people who lived on the earth, to figure out how to get into trouble. Satan, in the guise of a serpent, made them jealous of God's power. Satan suggested that they could have that power, too. All they had to do was reach for the forbidden fruit which grew on the forbidden tree. Adam and Eve actually believed Satan's lie; they thought that they, the creatures, could be as powerful and as wise and immortal as their creator. They thought that all that they had to do was eat of that special fruit. They did eat the special fruit, and in that act they violated, they broke, the relationship God had originally established between Him and them. Part of the breaking of that relationship meant that the life which they had received from Him was now also in jeopardy. They were in danger of losing it. Indeed, they would lose it. Like Humpty Dumpty who sat on a wall, they, too, had a great fall.

Capital punishment is when a person is executed for a certain crime. Do you think that the sentence of death for sinning is capital punishment? If so, do you think that it is fair? Is it that God sentences to death, or is it that we, by our sinning, have pulled away from our source of life (that we have broken our lifeline)? Who then is responsible for our dying?

❖ ❖ ❖ ❖ ❖

The rebellion of Adam and Eve against God (their "fall") is called "sin." And as the Scriptures tell us, "The wages of sin is death ... The soul that sins shall die" (Romans 6:23 and Ezekiel 18:20). That is not very good news. Nevertheless, we cannot argue with it. It simply is the way it is. Everybody since Adam and Eve has sinned and has consequently died or is going to die.

(There are two exceptions: according to the Scriptures, there were two men who did not see death. For some special reason God took both Enoch and Elijah directly to heaven. For an answer to the question "Why them and not someone else — or me, or you?" we'll have to wait until we get to heaven.)

There are many kinds of sins, and there are various degrees of sin. Identify some of these kinds and degrees of sins. Pay specific attention to the social consequences of some sins. Therefore, there are also different kinds and degrees of punishment. Are there any kinds of sins which are so private that they have no effect on the rest of society?

❖ ❖ ❖ ❖ ❖

Sin simply has broken life. It simply has destroyed that which God had so carefully made. Sin brought and continues to bring death. In the face of this grim prospect is there hope for us anywhere?

❖ ❖ ❖ ❖ ❖
Discuss death as punishment for sin and death as the consequence of sin.
❖ ❖ ❖ ❖ ❖

Even Saint Paul moans, "O wretched man that I am. Who shall deliver me from the body of this death?" (Romans 7:24). Who can save us from having participated in the eating of the forbidden fruit? Can the words, "Dust thou art, and unto dust thou shalt return," ever be reversed, turned around? Can we be delivered from the awful consequence of sin (which is death)? Is that possible?

❖ ❖ ❖ ❖ ❖
If the cause of death is removed, what will be the consequences? Why then do people still die? Are there two kinds of death, one in time and one for eternity? Describe and define the two. Are there also two kinds of living? One in time and one for eternity? Describe and define the two. (Refer to John 11:25-26.)
❖ ❖ ❖ ❖ ❖

"Thanks be to God who has given us the victory through Jesus Christ our Lord" (Romans 7:25). This is Jesus, who died our death on the cross so that we might live with Him. He died our death so that we might live His life. That is quite a trade, quite a bargain, for us. We give Him our death so that we might have His life. It is by Christ's sacrifice on the cross of Calvary that the eternal consequences of our sins have been removed.

Listen once more to the triumphant confession of Saint Paul: "O death, where is thy victory? O death, where is thy sting? ... Thanks be to God, who gives us the victory through our Lord Jesus Christ" (1 Corinthians 15:55-57).

What do you think about that?

Perhaps you are thinking, "What does this have to do with communion, with eating bread and drinking wine? Are you implying that if I eat the bread and drink the wine of the Sacrament that then I am never going to die? Is this some sort of magical bread and wine which can make me live forever? Is this the mystical Fountain of Youth?"

Well, I don't want to call it magical bread and wine, and certainly at the Altar we do not find the mythical Fountain of Youth, but here is the bread and wine of eternal life for us. Here can be found the answer to the greatest need we all have, the need to do something about death and dying. And there is only one way to have that need taken care of, and that is by having our sins forgiven. And that is exactly what partaking of Holy Communion is all about.

True, none of us has any chance at all of living forever here on earth. Ever since it was put on a tilt during the days of Adam and Eve we all are only pilgrims passing through. None of us has here an abiding home. But now we are destined to be with God forever. That is what Jesus meant when He promised, "I am the resurrection and the life; he who believes in me, though he die, yet shall he live, and whoever lives and believes in me shall never die" (John 11:25-26).

Those are some powerful words, and they give us a good reason for coming to the altar to receive the body and blood of Jesus "in, with, and under" the bread and wine of Holy Communion for the forgiveness of our sins. It is that forgiveness which carries with it the promise of life and salvation. That means that our lives which have been broken away from God are restored to and with Him once again. We are once more joined to Him who is the very source of life.

We are back to eating again. Nourishment for the body comes from food which is ingested. Nourishment for the soul must also be ingested. In a real, touchable, and tastable way we receive that which is necessary for life. Do you think that life would be just as real if God merely said so, if He merely made us a promise? What is the benefit of having the word come to us in the touchable and tastable form of Holy Communion?

It is interesting that even as death came by eating, now life also comes by eating. No wonder then that the Christian church makes so much of the Sacrament of Holy Communion. Here is life everlasting, and that is exactly what all of our hearts yearn for and need the most. Therefore, the Savior calls, "Come unto me, all you that labor and are heavy laden, and I will set you free from the fear of death; I will give you rest. I will give you a new lease on life."

Yes, our Lord has prepared quite a banquet for us, a banquet of life for life.

Questions

1. What must there be for everything that we do?

2. Why partake of Holy Communion?

3. What has sin done to our relationship with God?

4. How is that relationship restored?

Discussion

1. Discuss common things that you do but for which you sometimes are no longer aware of the reason for doing them.

2. If eating and drinking are for staying alive, comment on the frequency of receiving Holy Communion.

Holy Communion — The Sacrament Of The Altar: Part Three

In the last two chapters ("The Sacrament Of The Altar: Parts One and Two") we talked about such reason-defying subjects as the Real Presence of Christ's Body and Blood in the bread and wine of Holy Communion and life eternal even though we die. We said that all of this was possible because of the power of God's Word. Martin Luther was very tuned into and appreciated the power of God's Word. Review once again all the things that you can think of which are dependent upon the power of God's Word. What are all the things which God's Word does? (Remember that the words "word" and "verb" are related. What does that tell you?)

Not by all the bombs that have ever been dropped … not by all the bulldozers that have ever moved mountains … not by all the forces of nature put together, but by the power of the word, the word spoken, has more landscape on the horizon of human history been altered and rearranged than by any other force.

Noah Webster, the father of the American dictionary, said, "If I had to forfeit all the gifts with which I was endowed by my creator, but was permitted to retain just one of them, I would choose to hold onto the gift of speech. For with it I would regain everything else which I had lost." So powerful is the word!

❖ ❖ ❖ ❖ ❖
There is much power in a human's word also. Review some of the things which are the result of a human's word. There is, however, a difference between the power of God's Word and the power of a human's word. What are some of those differences? Which one is more dependable?
❖ ❖ ❖ ❖ ❖

It is THE WORD which empowers God's gift of Holy Communion.

And so we come to the third question that Dr. Martin Luther asks about The Sacrament of the Altar in the *Small Catechism*. The question is, "How can bodily eating and drinking do such great things?" (How can it deliver what was promised in the answer to the second question, namely, the forgiveness of sins, life, and salvation?) Here is Luther's answer:

> *Certainly not just eating and drinking do these things, but the words written here: "Given and shed for you for the forgiveness of sins." These words, along with the bodily eating and drinking, are the main thing in the Sacrament. Whoever believes these words has exactly what they say: "forgiveness of sins."*

How is it possible that eating and drinking, receiving Holy Communion, can do such great things? That is the question. From where does the power to give us what is promised come? Answer: from The Word, the powerful Word of God.

God's Word is powerful. "In the beginning God said ... and it was so." That is how creation took place. God said, "Let there be light ... and there was light." God said, "Let there be some stars over there, and some planets over there ... And how about a few trees? And now some birds for those trees, and some animals to play beneath those trees." God said, and it was so. When God spoke, a whole world listened and was not disappointed. That is because not only is God's Word so strong, but it is also dependable.

❖ ❖ ❖ ❖ ❖
Sometimes people confuse the idea of the "incarnation" with "reincarnation." What is the difference between the two? Which one is for real, and which one is only fantasy? What proof do we have of the one? What proof do we have of the other?
❖ ❖ ❖ ❖ ❖

For years and years, decades, generations, and centuries, God spoke a word of promise. He said that a Messiah would someday be born who would redeem humankind from the terrible consequences of their sins. Then, in the fullness of time, that "Word became flesh, and actually dwelt among us, and we beheld His glory, glory as of the only begotten Son of the Father, full of grace and truth" (John 1). That was the same Word which was there in the beginning. That was the same Word by which the entire universe was created. The Word! God! Powerful! Dependable! "In the beginning was the Word, and the Word was with God, and the Word was God; all things were made through Him, and without Him was not anything made that was made" (John 1:1-3).

"Word pollution" is the same as cheap talk, talk that doesn't mean what it says. Give some examples of "word pollution." Does "talk" need to be followed by action? What does "walk your talk" mean?
❖ ❖ ❖ ❖ ❖

These days we have the tendency to play down "the word." "Words are cheap," we are often tempted to say. And we often hear that "sticks and stones may break my bones, but words (names) can never harm me." That is not true. That is not true at all. Instead, is it not true that more hurt is done around your house by the ill words people speak to each other than by anything else? Also, is it not true that more good happens in your house, among your friends and so forth, by good and encouraging words that you speak to each other than by anything else? A biting, critical remark hurts more than a punch in the eye. And a compliment or "thank you" lasts longer than an embrace or a hug. That is because our words come from within; they come from where is found the very source of life. Indeed, more landscape on the horizon of human history has been altered and rearranged by what people have said than by anything else people have done.

Are you having a good day or a bad day? Do you see any connection between the kind of day you are having and the kinds of words that have been spoken to you since you got up in the morning? Let's "put the shoe on the other foot." What have your words done to other people today? Have they helped to build them up, or have they tended to tear them down?

It seems that people in Bible times were much more sensitive to this than we are today. To them words seemed much more alive. For example, when a curse was hurdled in someone's direction, that person might very well duck. He would duck in order to avoid being hit by those negative words which could do to him great damage. Likewise, when a benediction was said, when those good words were sent in the direction of someone, the person on the receiving end might very well stand upright with arms wide open in hope of catching the good power from them. Perhaps that is why to this day when the benediction is spoken by the pastor at the end of a worship service the congregation stands up. The members of the congregation want to catch the blessing and take it along with them out into the world for the rest of the week.

❖ ❖ ❖ ❖ ❖
You have probably heard it said (or something similar). "It might not sound very pretty, but I just say it like it is." What do you think about that expression? Do you think we ought to always be careful about "the way we say a thing"? Do you think that it is true that if we are not careful about our words that then we are not careful about a lot of things?
❖ ❖ ❖ ❖ ❖

I think that if we were all more sensitive to the power of words, we would both be more careful in using words that can hurt and try harder to say good things to one another.

The point in all of this is that God's word of promise in the Sacrament of Holy Communion offers a mighty big blessing — the forgiveness of sins, life, and salvation. It is His Word which makes all of this possible, that Word which says that "in, with, and under" the very bread and wine of Communion are the body and the blood of Jesus the Christ, who gave Himself as a sacrifice upon the cross for us.

Now it is for us to trust this Word, this powerful Word of God. We by faith can jump into it. By faith we trust that Word which tells us that here is the Body and the Blood of Jesus for the forgiveness of our sins and which then delivers all the blessings that follow.

❖ ❖ ❖ ❖ ❖
Trust is a very powerful force also. What are some examples of trust? What is the result of trust? How important of a role does trusting play in making something happen? Why do we sometimes not trust? What must be necessary for us to be trusting? Is God very trustworthy? Cite examples from the Bible of people who trusted what God promised. (For example, Daniel in the lions' den. The Psalms also are rich in examples of trusting.) What was the result of such trusting? If you were blindfolded, whom would you trust to take you by the hand and lead you? If blind people didn't trust their "seeing eye dogs," what would happen? If airplane and ship navigators didn't trust their instruments (like the compass), what would be the result?
❖ ❖ ❖ ❖ ❖

That reminds us that participating in Holy Communion, receiving the Sacrament, is not some sort of mind game. No! It is an action. It is something that we do, and in the doing we touch that which is real. The same can be said about what Jesus did for us on Calvary. Our salvation is not built upon some sort of philosophical principle; it is built upon an act. God in a very real way worked out our salvation by sending His Son right down here to our earth. Yes, He was up to His neck in the dust of this world. Our salvation was accomplished by something which happened. That something is historical. It is documented. If there had been video cameras in those days, it could all have been recorded on tape. So also our getting in touch with the Christ of Calvary is not just something which happens in our minds. Jesus is not just an idea or a feeling. And by the actual eating of the Communion bread and drinking from the Communion cup we are in touch with Jesus and with what happened for us some 2,000 years ago some 6,000 miles away.

Nevertheless, these words of promise are good for us only if we believe them, if we put our trust in them. We can call this action of believing a "leap of faith." We trust that what God says He will deliver. We can take Him at His Word.

❖ ❖ ❖ ❖ ❖
In what way is participating in Holy Communion a "leap of faith," an act of trusting? Whom are we trusting? What are we trusting?
❖ ❖ ❖ ❖ ❖

Therefore, we do what He invites us to do. In Luke 14 (and also in Matthew 22) Jesus tells the parable about a rich man who prepared a great banquet. All the finest fare imaginable was to be served. When all was ready he sent out invitations to his friends, relatives, and neighbors. He wanted to treat them all to a great feast. But all too many had excuses for not coming. One had just bought a new business. One had to go shopping. One had just been married. Thus for one reason or another they did not think that participating in the feast was worth it. Consequently, they did not accept the invitation. They never found out what treats were in store for them. They never got in on the action. Only those who responded, who trusted the invitation, who really thought that the party would be great, only they found out what good things awaited them. Those who had excuses were left out in the cold.

❖ ❖ ❖ ❖ ❖
When someone extends to you an invitation, how can you "get in on the action"? God is a God of action. How can we get in on His action? God's action is narrated in His story. How can we get in on His story? Excuses stand in the way of getting in on the action/story. What seems more reasonable: the invitation or the excuses?
❖ ❖ ❖ ❖ ❖

(Do you know what excuses are? They are reasons for not making something happen. And, by the way, those who are good at making excuses usually are also good at blaming. Do you know what blaming is? It is not wanting to accept responsibility for what has happened.)

God invites us to be people of faith, people of action, people who trust His Word which makes things happen.

❖ ❖ ❖ ❖ ❖

A kiss is the physical side or sign of the words, "I love you." Do you think that Holy Communion is a physical side or sign of God's love toward us? What is physical about it? What does it have to do with love?

❖ ❖ ❖ ❖ ❖

Finally, if I say "I love you" and you think that I don't mean it, or if you don't want my love, then those words will simply fall to the ground unrequited and will probably get kicked into a corner. On the other hand, if you really believe me when I say, "I love you," and if you really value being loved by me, then these words will have a profound effect upon you. They will significantly influence our relationship. If that is what happens between us because of our words, much more so is that true of God's Words spoken to us.

Listen again to Martin Luther reminding us, "Whoever believes these words has exactly what they say: the forgiveness of sins." Such is the power of God's Word. Such is what happens when we believe it, trust it, and jump into it.

Questions

1. What is the most powerful force in the whole world?

2. What are some of the ways in which we have been made aware of the powerful Word of God?

3. Why do some people think that it is important to stand when words of benediction are spoken in their direction?

4. What is a "leap of faith"?

5. Instead of accepting God's Word of promise, what do we often do?

6. Who receives what the word of promise in Holy Communion promises?

Discussion

1. Discuss examples of words that hurt and of words that heal.

2. Give examples of life being affected by the trusting of words.

Holy Communion —
The Sacrament Of The Altar:
Part Four

❖ ❖ ❖ ❖ ❖
It is an exciting thing to get an invitation to an important event or from an important person. What are some of the more exciting invitations you have received? Who did the inviting and what was the occasion? Did you engage in any kind of preparations for your attendance at the event? What was the nature of some of those preparations? Were those preparations important? Were they necessary?
❖ ❖ ❖ ❖ ❖

Would you like an invitation for dinner at the White House with the President? I certainly would consider it to be a great honor if such an invitation would come to me. I think you would too.

There is an even greater invitation which carries an even greater honor. It is the invitation our Lord makes, saying to us, "Come, for all has been prepared. The banquet is ready. Come and dine." This is His invitation to gather around His altar in order to receive the Sacrament of the Altar, Holy Communion, the Eucharist.

Certainly, if we would accept an invitation to have dinner with the President we would make careful preparations for the event. There would undoubtedly be shining of the shoes, combing of the hair, and a brushing up on manners, etiquette, and so forth. Would you not then think that such care and preparation should be applied also when accepting an invitation to appear at the altar of the Lord in order to receive Holy Communion? Yes, proper preparation certainly is in order.

Our instruction on preparation in this matter comes from Saint Paul. In particular he addressed this issue in the 11th chapter of his first letter to the Corinthians. Things had gotten rather out of hand in Corinth at communion time. Communion, you see, with the early Christians was oftentimes part of a large meal called the "agape" meal. The word "agape" means "love." Back in those days there were no such things as pensions or savings accounts or Medicare or welfare; there were no such things as Social Security or IRAs. That meant that if you were old and did not have children to take care of you, you were in trouble. The same also applied to widows and young children and the disabled. If you could not take care of yourself, and if you did not have family members who would take care of you, then you were literally "down and out." In that respect life was a lot more cruel then than it is today.

Looking out for one another, caring for one another, always seem to have been an important part of a Christian congregation's life. How important is it to your congregation? How is it carried out? Do you have any part in it?

Therefore, Christians developed the custom of having a great big potluck meal of sorts every Sunday, their day of worship when they honored the resurrected Lord. To this meal all those who had an abundance of good things to eat were expected to bring a lot so that everybody in the congregation could eat well. After the meal was over, the leftovers were distributed to those who could not provide for themselves. Thus the poor, the disabled, the elderly, and the young children without parents would all have at least one good meal a week and could take home with them food for the rest of the week. Yes, this was a "love feast," an "agape meal." It was a meal of sharing.

The Sharing (Agape) Meal and the Communion Meal were closely associated with one another in the early church. Why was that so? Would it be good if the same were true today? Why would it be good? What conditions have changed in our society that have led to the separation of those two kinds of meals? Does that mean that the church no longer has the responsibility to look after one another? How can the church still serve the needs of those in need?

At the heart of this meal was the celebration of Holy Communion. Some of the bread and some of the wine was consecrated, set aside from the rest. It became the means whereby the people would not only remember God's great love for them in the sacrifice of Jesus, but they actually got in touch with the body and the blood of their Savior through the miracle of this Sacrament. The agape meal with Holy Communion at its heart is a demonstration of how God out of love provides both for the hunger of people's bodies and their souls.

❖ ❖ ❖ ❖ ❖
Do you see a connection between the abuses that accompanied the agape meal in Corinth and members of a church in our time not being concerned about the welfare of the needy?
❖ ❖ ❖ ❖ ❖

But all did not always go well in Corinth. There were some people who behaved terribly at the meal. They loaded their plates with absolutely no consideration for whether or not there would be enough for everybody. In addition, some of the big and strong ones pushed their weight around. Meanwhile, those who needed the meal the most were often shoved aside or to the end of the line. If that were not bad enough, this kind of behavior flowed over into the communion portion of the meal also. Thus some stuffed their faces with the bread, and some even got drunk on the wine. Paul, appalled by such behavior, scolded the Corinthians. He said, "Don't you people know what you are doing? This is the Lord's body and blood involved here."

> *Whoever, therefore, eats the bread or drinks the cup of the Lord in an unworthy manner will be guilty of profaning the body and blood of the Lord. Let a man examine himself, and so eat of the bread and drink of the cup. For anyone who eats and drinks without discerning the body eats and drinks judgment upon himself.* —1 Corinthians 11:27-39

Let a person examine himself, herself, and then eat the bread and drink the wine of Holy Communion.

❖ ❖ ❖ ❖ ❖
The word "profane" means "to be abused or cheapened" or "to be treated rudely." Do we profane Jesus when we treat one another rudely, when we are abusive of one another? (Refer to Matthew 25:42-45.)
❖ ❖ ❖ ❖ ❖

You might ask, "Just what does the word 'examine' suggest?"

Ultimately, it means to make sure you are taking the Sacrament for the right reasons.

❖ ❖ ❖ ❖ ❖
Right reasons and proper motives are important. Think of some kind of action which could be done either for right or for wrong reasons (for example, helping somebody out because you want to get paid for it or simply because they need some help).
❖ ❖ ❖ ❖ ❖

Are you doing it because everybody else is doing it? (That's not a right reason.)

Are you doing it because pressure is being brought to bear upon you to do it? (That is not a right reason.)

Are you coming to the altar without really knowing what is going on? (That is not right or good.)

❖ ❖ ❖ ❖ ❖
Some people say that they don't take communion because they are so ashamed of their sins. Some people say that some should not take communion because of the seriousness of their sins. What does Jesus say in Matthew 9:12 about this?
❖ ❖ ❖ ❖ ❖

We should, however, partake of Holy Communion because we know that we have a great need for it. That is a good and a right reason. Therefore, we partake of Holy Communion because we acknowledge that we are sinners. Jesus made His sacrifice on the cross because we are sinners.

I suggest to the students of my catechism classes that if they doubt that they are sinners all that they need to do is look at their lives against the standards of the Ten Commandments and compare their lives to them. How are you doing? For example —

The First Commandment: "You shall have no other gods." Is God really always #1 in your life? Or do you place work or pleasure first and God second, third, or even fourth, to be called on only in extreme situations?

The Fourth Commandment: "Honor your father and mother." Have you been disrespectful toward your parents or to others in authority?

The Seventh Commandment: "You shall not steal." Have you misrepresented goods in selling or trading? Have you taken that which did not belong to you?

The Eighth Commandment: "You shall not give false testimony against your neighbor." Have you always spoken the best you could about others, or have you gossiped and so forth?

If we are honest with ourselves, we all must admit that we have broken the commandments — every one of them. That is what we call sin — breaking the commandments. In that breaking we see our sin, and in that respect the commandments are like mirrors to us. They reflect back to us so that we can see the wrong which we have done or the right which we have not done. It is precisely for that kind of behavior, for those sins, that Jesus died on the cross so that we might have forgiveness.

❖ ❖ ❖ ❖ ❖
For what kind of people did Jesus die? (Refer to Romans 5:6-8.) For what kind of people was the Sacrament of Holy Communion instituted? When is a person properly prepared to receive this sacrament? What is the nature of his or her preparation? What kind of examination is called for in this regard?
❖ ❖ ❖ ❖ ❖

After such an examination of oneself, it is good to say, "I need Jesus; I need what He has done for me." Therefore, proper examination and preparation for receiving Holy Communion involves knowing why we are receiving communion and why the bread and the wine of this sacrament are what is just right for our problem.

That then brings us to the fourth and final question in the communion section of Dr. Martin Luther's *Small Catechism*: Who receives this sacrament worthily? And the answer:

Fasting and bodily preparation are certainly fine outward training. But that person is truly worthy and well prepared who has faith in these words: "Given and shed for you for the forgiveness of sins."

But anyone who does not believe these words or doubts them is unworthy and unprepared, for the words "for you" require all hearts to believe.

That is what makes us properly prepared. That is what it means to examine oneself.

Although not required by the Bible, what would you suggest as some other good things to do in preparation for receiving the Sacrament of the Altar? What do you consider proper behavior, decorum, and etiquette for receiving the Sacrament? Do you think that you should hold other people to these standards?

Again, receiving Holy Communion is a "leap of faith." What is the object of that faith? How much trust is involved? If a person has some doubts, if the trust is not 100 percent, do you think that person should stay away from this Sacrament? Do you think that having the proper motive or reason, even if there is some doubt or even if faith is weak, is sufficient for approaching the altar to receive Holy Communion?
❖ ❖ ❖ ❖ ❖

One final comment about preparing oneself to receive Holy Communion. We should be careful not to think that we are worthy of receiving the Sacrament only when we have made ourselves "clean" enough, only when we have prepared enough, only when our examination has uncovered every last detail of our sins. Because, you see, if we have made ourselves good enough, then we have no need for communion. If we have nothing left which needs to be forgiven, then there is no sense in partaking of this Sacrament of Forgiveness.

❖ ❖ ❖ ❖ ❖
In one simple sentence express when it is that a person is properly prepared to receive the Sacrament of Holy Communion.
❖ ❖ ❖ ❖ ❖

Jesus said that He came for the sick, not for those who have no need of a doctor. He came for sinners, not for those who think that they already have made themselves righteous. In other words, Holy Communion is not for those who no longer have a need for it — if there really are any such people. It is for those who have a great need and who know it and who know where to turn to have that need met.

❖ ❖ ❖ ❖ ❖
In the matter of Faith and Life why is it appropriate to give God all the credit and glory?
❖ ❖ ❖ ❖ ❖

Questions

1. What had gone wrong in Corinth during Paul's time?

2. What were the purposes of the agape meal?

3. What are some wrong reasons for approaching the altar to receive the Sacrament?

4. What are some of the right reasons for approaching the altar to receive the Sacrament?

5. Who then is worthy to receive the Sacrament?

Discussion

1. Discuss good habits that could be cultivated for preparing to receive the Sacraments of the Altar.

2. Discuss feelings of unworthiness with regards to receiving the Sacrament of the Altar.

www.ingramcontent.com/pod-product-compliance
Lightning Source LLC
Chambersburg PA
CBHW080455170426
43196CB00016B/2820